PRESENTED TO:

FROM:

DATE:

180 DEVOTIONS TO SPARK YOUR FAITH

RENAE BRUMBAUGH GREEN

180 DEVOTIONS TO SPARK YOUR FAITH

Abundant Inspiration for Women

© 2025 by Barbour Publishing, Inc.

Print ISBN 979-8-89151-076-0

All rights reserved. No part of this publication may be reproduced or transmitted for commercial purposes, except for brief quotations in printed reviews, without written permission of the publisher. Reproduced text may not be used on the World Wide Web. No Barbour Publishing content may be used as artificial intelligence training data for machine learning, or in any similar software development.

Churches and other noncommercial interests may reproduce portions of this book without the express written permission of Barbour Publishing, provided that the text does not exceed 500 words or 5 percent of the entire book, whichever is less, and that the text is not material quoted from another publisher. When reproducing text from this book, include the following credit line: "From *180 Devotions to Spark Your Faith: Abundant Inspiration for Women*, published by Barbour Publishing, Inc. Used by permission."

All scripture quotations, unless otherwise indicated, are from The ESV® Bible (The Holy Bible, English Standard Version®). ESV® Text Edition: 2016. Copyright © 2001 by Crossway, a publishing ministry of Good News Publishers. The ESV® text has been reproduced in cooperation with and by permission of Good News Publishers. Unauthorized reproduction of this publication is prohibited. All rights reserved.

Scripture quotations marked NASB are taken from the New American Standard Bible®, Copyright © 1960, 1971, 1977, 1995, 2020 by The Lockman Foundation. All rights reserved.

Scripture quotations marked NIV are taken from THE HOLY BIBLE, NEW INTERNATIONAL VERSION®. NIV®. Copyright © 1973, 1978, 1984, 2011 by Biblica, Inc.® Used by permission. All rights reserved worldwide.

Scripture quotations marked NLT are taken from the *Holy Bible*, New Living Translation copyright © 1996, 2004, 2015 by Tyndale House Foundation. Used by permission of Tyndale House Publishers, Inc. Carol Stream, Illinois 60188. All rights reserved.

Cover image © Greg Jackson, Thinkpen Design

Published by Barbour Publishing, Inc., 1810 Barbour Drive, Uhrichsville, Ohio 44683, www.barbourbooks.com

Our mission is to inspire the world with the life-changing message of the Bible.

Printed in China.

Many years ago, when my children were small, we got them a go-cart for Christmas. They zoomed and squealed and made the best memories on their grandparents' country acreage until one day, it stopped working. Turns out, it needed a new spark plug. A quick trip to the mechanic, and it was good as new.

I remember looking at that go-cart and thinking, *I can relate. I'm tired. I feel like my spark has gone.* As with that go-cart, my answer lay with the Mechanic. The missing spark was God's Word. During that busy time in my life, I'd neglected spending time with God.

The more time we spend with our Father, the more we soak in His presence, the more energized we become. He infuses us with His peace, His strength, His joy, His patience, and His love. And the more we meditate on His Word—the sword of the Spirit—the sharper our swords become as we grow into His powerful warrior-daughters.

Are you missing your spark? Join me on this journey into God's promises, and see how they rekindle your faith, spur your energy, and ignite the light of His love in your life.

Renae

FERTILE FAITH

The law of the Lord is perfect, reviving the soul; the testimony of the Lord is sure, making wise the simple; the precepts of the Lord are right, rejoicing the heart; the commandment of the Lord is pure, enlightening the eyes; the fear of the Lord is clean, enduring forever; the rules of the Lord are true, and righteous altogether. More to be desired are they than gold, even much fine gold; sweeter also than honey and drippings of the honeycomb. Moreover, by them is your servant warned; in keeping them there is great reward.

PSALM 19:7–11

Modern society wants us to believe that faith is a personal thing that's different for each of us. While that is somewhat true, because God created each of us to have a unique and personal relationship with Him, His basic truths don't change. If we want our faith in God to grow, we must start with His Word. When we read God's words, we learn His wisdom, His character, His passion. In His Word, we find His heart.

Listen to Him by reading His Word. Talk to Him in prayer. The more we get to know our Father, the more amazed and humbled we are by His love. The process of knowing God is the fertilizer that causes our faith to grow strong.

Thank You for giving me access to Your Word,
Father. I know it holds the key to Your heart. I want
to know You more. I want my faith to be strong.
As much as possible, I want to be just like You.

LIGHT

*The Lord is my light and my salvation;
whom shall I fear? The Lord is the stronghold
of my life; of whom shall I be afraid?*
Psalm 27:1

If modern US citizens had to choose one word as our theme or motto, it might be the word *freedom*. For the ancient Hebrews, that word was *light*. To call something a light means it is a source of joy, knowledge, and understanding. For David—and for us—God is our light.

God was also the source of David's salvation. He certainly saved David from some precarious situations, and He promises to do the same for us. Moreover, God was David's stronghold, or safe place. With God, there was no need to fear.

God is the same today as He was in David's time. He adores His people—which means He adores *you*. He wants to be the source of your joy. He wants to be your safe place. And He holds out His arms, ready to be your salvation. Whatever you're facing, trust Him with the outcome. He loves you more than anything, and He will never let you go.

Father, You know what I'm facing right now. You know my faith is weak. I'm having trouble trusting You in this. Like David, I want to experience Your light. I want to feel the safety of Your presence. I need You to save me. Even when it's hard, I choose to trust You. I know You are good.

SEEK HIM

"When I shut up the heavens so that there is no rain, or command the locust to devour the land, or send pestilence among my people, if my people who are called by my name humble themselves, and pray and seek my face and turn from their wicked ways, then I will hear from heaven and will forgive their sin and heal their land."

2 CHRONICLES 7:13–14

Our actions have consequences—some good, some bad. But God finds no pleasure in our pain. He loves us more than we love ourselves, and to see us hurting breaks His heart.

Sometimes our own guilt keeps us from calling out to God. We think we deserve whatever we're going through, so we distance ourselves from God instead of running to Him. If we only understood how God waits for us, how He longs for our presence, how He stands ready—arms wide, waiting to embrace us in His love—we wouldn't hesitate. All we have to say is "God, I'm sorry. God, I need You. God, help!" and He is right there.

More than anything, He wants to heal your heart. He wants to restore your relationship with Him. What's holding you back? Call out to Him today and sink deep into His love.

Lord, I'm sorry for the mess I've made. I'm stuck here. . . . I can't get myself out. I need You. You are my only hope. Help me, Lord. I long to please You. I want to live for You.

PEACE

"Peace I leave with you; my peace I give to you. Not as the world gives do I give to you. Let not your hearts be troubled, neither let them be afraid."
JOHN 14:27

When we think of peace, many of us picture a beachside oasis, lounging in the sand with a book and a glass of peach-flavored iced tea. While that sounds amazing, it wouldn't last. Eventually, we'd realize we're covered in a million grains of sand that stick to our shoes, our cars, and our carpets. We might even get a sunburn.

God's peace has nothing to do with location or situation. His peace is embedded in our hearts, and we carry it with us everywhere. We don't have to wait for the next vacation or the next promotion or the next *whatever* to find it. We already have it.

But many of us forget it's there. We forget to access it. Do you need peace right now? Look to God. Ask Him to show you His presence. Cling to His love. Pour out your heart to Him. Before you know it, you'll feel a peace that defies understanding. And it's been there all along, ready for you to grab hold.

Father, right now my life feels like a hurricane. But I know things feel peaceful in the eye of the hurricane. I'm going to center myself in You and wait for the peace You've already given me.

FEAR NOT

Fear not, for I am with you; be not dismayed,
for I am your God; I will strengthen you, I will help you,
I will uphold you with my righteous right hand.

ISAIAH 41:10

A recent survey showed that more than 300 million people worldwide suffer from an anxiety disorder. That makes anxiety the most common mental health issue in the world. Add to that the number of people who suffer without a diagnosis, and you end up with a lot of people who are perpetually worried or afraid. But 2 Timothy 1:7 tells us that fear isn't from God.

Experts disagree on the exact number of times "Fear not" appears in the Bible, but all agree it's in there at least a hundred times. Some say the phrase is represented in various forms over three hundred times. That's a lot of reminders not to be afraid!

The truth is, we are God's children, made in His image. He is powerful, and His power lives in us. He is strong and confident, and so are we. He promises good things to those who love Him, and that leaves us full of hope.

Whatever it is that makes you feel anxious or afraid, give it to God. Trust Him to make beauty from ashes. Believe in His love for you and take hold of His strength. He adores you, and He will never let you down.

Thank You for this reminder not to be afraid, Lord. Remind me of the strength You've placed in me. I trust Your love.

ASK FOR WISDOM

*I sought the L*ORD*, and he answered me
and delivered me from all my fears.*
PSALM 34:4

Just before David wrote this psalm, he had escaped death as Abimelech pursued him. David cried out to God, and God showed him what to do to get away. Interestingly, it involved David pretending to be insane, because neither Abimelech nor the Philistines who pursued David wanted anything to do with an insane person. They believed contact with such a person would bring curses.

Crazy story, right? Yet God is all-knowing and all-wise. When we seek Him for answers, He often provides ideas and solutions we wouldn't have thought of ourselves. What hard thing do you face right now? What unknown future circumstance leaves you worried, perplexed, and scratching your head? Ask God for wisdom. He will always answer those who sincerely seek Him.

James 1:5 tells us He *generously* gives wisdom to those who ask. Too often we look in the wrong places for solutions to our problems. We read psychology books or self-help books. We rely on money or education or status to solve our dilemmas. But none of those is foolproof. God's wisdom will always lead us to truth, kindness, and love. And it will help us become the strong, wise, fearless people He created us to be.

You know what I'm facing right now, Lord. Like David, I don't see a way out. But just as You showed David a solution, I know You'll provide me with the wisdom and resources I need to get through this. I trust You completely.

THE FORMULA

Do not be anxious about anything, but in everything by prayer and supplication with thanksgiving let your requests be made known to God. And the peace of God, which surpasses all understanding, will guard your hearts and your minds in Christ Jesus.

PHILIPPIANS 4:6–7

This passage contains a lot of absolutes: Don't be anxious about *anything*. Pray about *everything*. Peace that defies *all* understanding will guard us.

Paul didn't say, "Try not to be anxious" or "If all else fails, try praying" or "Peace might come if you're lucky." The formula here is definite and unchanging.

We'll feel anxiety because we're human. But we're not supposed to *be* anxious. That means we choose not to sit in that anxiety. When it shows up, we know how to get rid of it: through prayer and thanksgiving!

When we focus on our anxieties, we take our eyes off God. But when we take our fears and stresses to God, we put our eyes back on Him. When we thank Him for all He's done and all we know He's going to do, our thoughts shift from our circumstances to God's goodness.

That doesn't mean He'll answer every prayer the way we want Him to. He has a great plan, and He's not obligated to let us in on what He's doing. But He promises His peace. It's a peace that doesn't make sense to those who don't know Him. But it's a peace that enfolds and comforts us, even when our circumstances don't make sense.

I give it all to You, Lord. Thank You for Your peace.

THE ONE WHO GOES BEFORE YOU

"It is the Lord who goes before you. He will be with you; he will not leave you or forsake you. Do not fear or be dismayed."
Deuteronomy 31:8

Whether in the movies or in real life, a person's last words are often powerful and significant. In this passage, Moses is 120 years old. He knows he will die soon, and he's giving a big speech, reminding the Israelites of all the important things. Then, in a moment filled with drama and expectation, he calls Joshua to stand beside him. In front of everyone, Moses passes the baton to Joshua. He was to take over where Moses left off.

This verse tells us what Moses said to his protégé. These words, recorded in God's Word, can be applied to each of our lives as well. God—who is not bound by calendars or time—goes before us. With anything we face, we can know God has already been there, preparing the way. He also stands beside us, holding our hand, guiding us. Since He's already been there, He knows the way.

We have *nothing* to fear. Our Father is for us. He goes before us. And He walks beside us.

It's hard for me to understand how You could go before me into the future, Father. But that's what faith is, isn't it? I know You love me, and I know You've prepared the way for me to travel this road. Thank You for walking beside me through it all.

THE GOOD SHEPHERD

Even though I walk through the valley of the shadow of death, I will fear no evil, for you are with me; your rod and your staff, they comfort me.

PSALM 23:4

Experts believe Psalm 23—one of the most memorized passages of scripture—was composed near the end of David's life. As he contemplated death, he knew, based on his past experience, that he had nothing to fear. He knew that nothing could separate him from his Father's presence.

The same is true for us. Whether we face death, financial ruin, physical ailments, or family turmoil, God will never leave us. We have nothing to fear. We could say that even though I walk through the valley of teen drivers or even though I walk through the valley of a stressful, toxic work environment, *I will fear no evil, for You are with me.*

The rod and staff were shepherd's tools. The rod was used for defense and for discipline when needed. The staff—a long stick with a crook—helped rescue sheep when they ended up in a precarious position. Those tools provide comfort to the sheep because they know the shepherd will take care of them. In the same way, we can be confident that God stands ready to defend us, guide us in the right way, and rescue us.

Thank You for being my good shepherd. I trust You completely.

FAITH

Now faith is the assurance of things hoped for, the conviction of things not seen.

HEBREWS 11:1

Some people who aren't familiar with the concept of faith may see it as a blind, illogical belief in something that isn't real. They may scoff at faith, believing it's no more than a fairy tale. But nothing could be further from the truth.

In the same way that we sit in a chair without examining it first or turn on our car's ignition believing it will start, faith is the logical belief that God is who He says He is. Yet while a chair may break and a car may not start, God will never, ever fail. He always keeps His promises. We know this will be true in the future because it has always been true in the past.

We have *assurance* that God loves us. He gave His Son to take the punishment we deserved for our sin—to pay the penalty we could never pay. This kind of commitment offers proof that He's all in. He will keep His Word. Just look at how He led the Israelites into the Promised Land, centuries after He made the promise to Abraham!

We can look back at our own lives and see the consistency of His character. He is always good, always kind, always loving. He always works things out for our good in the end. We can have faith in the future because we know the past. Faith in God is the most logical option we can choose.

Father, I know You are who You say You are. I trust You completely.

MOVED WITH PITY

And a leper came to him, imploring him, and kneeling said to him, "If you will, you can make me clean." Moved with pity, he stretched out his hand and touched him and said to him, "I will; be clean." And immediately the leprosy left him, and he was made clean.

MARK 1:40–42

Although it's rare today, people still get leprosy. But now there are effective treatments, so there's no need for quarantine. But in Jesus' time, a leprosy diagnosis meant long-term separation from family, friends, and community. As well as being quite painful, it was a shameful, lonely existence. When this leper sought out Jesus for help, Jesus was "moved with pity." Other words for pity are *compassion*, *sympathy*, and *sorrow*.

Jesus feels the same for us. When we come to Him, when we stretch out our hands and say, "If You will, You can help me," He is moved. He looks at us, sizes up our situation, and says, "I will help."

Though we may not understand His ways or His timing, we can be certain He loves us. He is moved with compassion over our plight. And He is already working on our behalf.

Father, I know You see what I'm going through. I can't help myself, but I know You can help me. Like the leper in this story, I'm reaching out to You in faith. Thank You for loving me and being moved by my pain.

IN HIS TIME

And Jesus sternly charged him and sent him away at once, and said to him, "See that you say nothing to anyone, but go, show yourself to the priest and offer for your cleansing what Moses commanded, for a proof to them." But he went out and began to talk freely about it, and to spread the news, so that Jesus could no longer openly enter a town, but was out in desolate places, and people were coming to him from every quarter.

MARK 1:43–45

It seems strange that Jesus didn't want the leper to tell anyone about his healing. You'd think Jesus would be eager for people to know who He was. But God's ways are higher than our ways. They don't always make sense in the moment. . .but His ways are always best.

Jesus knew He had a lot of work to do before His time on earth ended. He wanted a slow burn rather than a speedy spread. He needed time to travel farther, do more work, and reach more people. He needed time to teach His ways before He was overwhelmed with people just wanting miracles.

When God's timing doesn't make sense, trust Him anyway. He sees the bigger picture when we don't. We can be confident that no matter what, He is working things out for our good.

I don't understand what's happening in my life right now, Father, but I trust Your timing.

DIFFERENT SPIRITS

And whenever the unclean spirits saw him, they fell down before him and cried out, "You are the Son of God."
MARK 3:11

Have you ever met someone and immediately felt a kinship with them? It feels great to have that spirit-connection with another person. The opposite can be true too. We can barely know someone, but something about them makes us uncomfortable—and they may feel the same way about us. It's hard to explain that kind of subconscious like or dislike.

While there may be different reasons for those feelings, this passage supports the idea that spirits recognize other spirits. The unclean—or evil—spirits recognized Jesus. James 2:19 tells us, "Even the demons believe [in God]—and shudder!"

Evil recognizes and fears the presence of God. We are God's children, and His Spirit lives in us. It shouldn't be a surprise that when we're living for God, people who aren't honoring God don't like us. They will be uncomfortable in our presence. They may even go against us.

The truth is, they may not understand the reason for their disdain. That's okay. Keep living for God. Keep smiling, keep loving, keep sharing His light. His power in you will overcome the darkness.

Lord, it's hard living in a world where evil is celebrated and godliness is mocked. Even so, I want others to recognize Your Spirit in me. Help me to love like You love.

FAMILY PROBLEMS

Then he went home, and the crowd gathered again, so that they could not even eat. And when his family heard it, they went out to seize him, for they were saying, "He is out of his mind."
MARK 3:20–21

Imagine how hard it must have been to be Jesus' brother or sister. I mean, they watched Him grow up. They may have wrestled on the floor or had food fights with Him. They were too close to Him to see Him as special. And now He was out there, in public, telling people He was the Son of *God*?

When God does a great work in us, our families are often the most skeptical. Jesus had four brothers and at least two sisters (Matthew 13:55–56). At least two of them—James and Jude—became converts after Jesus' death. Those two wrote the books of the Bible named after them.

If your family doesn't understand what God is doing in your life, be patient. Be kind. Love them. But don't let them keep you from living out your authentic calling in Christ. God will use this hardship to shape you into who He wants you to be. And He'll use your faithfulness to draw them to Himself.

I think it's hardest to be godly, to be my best self, with my family. I need Your strength to respond to them with Your patience, kindness, and love. Help me, Father. I want them to know You the way I do.

PEACE! BE STILL!

And he awoke and rebuked the wind and said to the sea, "Peace! Be still!" And the wind ceased, and there was a great calm.

MARK 4:39

Jesus' disciples had spent a great deal of time with Him at this point. They'd watched Him heal the sick and cast out demons. They'd watched Him teach with wisdom that can only come from God. Yet here, in the middle of a storm, they panicked. The waves crashed, and the boat began to fill with water. When they found Jesus asleep, they got a little upset: "Don't You care that we're about to drown?"

The answer was no. He wasn't afraid. He had no reason to be. He commanded the winds and the seas, and they obeyed His orders. After He hushed the tempest, He asked His disciples, "Why are you so scared? Don't you have any faith by now?"

The same thing happens when we face storms. We watch our lives fill up with water, and we think we'll surely drown. We panic, and we cry out to Him—"Father! Don't You see what's happening?" Just as He calmed the literal storm in this passage, He will calm our spirits. He will hush the stress and anxiety. With a gentle voice, He'll say, "It's okay. Remember your faith. I have everything under control."

**I know You see the storms in my life, Father.
I trust You to calm the storm around me.
Thank You for giving me Your peace.**

TELL YOUR STORY

As he was getting into the boat, the man who had been possessed with demons begged him that he might be with him. And he did not permit him but said to him, "Go home to your friends and tell them how much the Lord has done for you, and how he has had mercy on you." And he went away and began to proclaim in the Decapolis how much Jesus had done for him, and everyone marveled.

MARK 5:18–20

Just as Jesus arrived onshore and stepped out of His boat, a man approached Him. This man was demon-possessed. He'd been living among the tombs. People had tried to subdue him by strapping or chaining him down, but he always broke free. He was tortured and miserable. He threw himself before Jesus, and the demons cried out in recognition.

When Jesus healed him, the man begged to go with Jesus and His disciples. But Jesus had a different job for this fellow. He said, "I'd rather you go and tell everyone you know what I've done for you."

We don't need a degree in theology or public speaking to make a difference for Christ. All He asks is that we tell our stories. He says to us the same thing He said to that man: "Go home to your friends and tell them how much the Lord has done for you."

Give me opportunities to talk about all the wonderful things You've done for me, Lord. . .and give me the words to say.

NOW AND LATER

And immediately the king sent an executioner with orders to bring John's head. He went and beheaded him in the prison and brought his head on a platter and gave it to the girl, and the girl gave it to her mother. When his disciples heard of it, they came and took his body and laid it in a tomb.

MARK 6:27–29

For most people, this isn't a passage we consider when we want to build our faith. After all, what a horrible ending! John spent his life serving his Lord, and this is the way he died? Where is the justice?

Sometimes we get the mistaken idea that if we live for God, our lives will be easy. We think it's some kind of divine trade-off. We please God, and He makes the way smooth for us. And yes, that does happen sometimes. But Christ told us in John 16:33 that in this world we will have trouble.

But that's the key: *in this world*. Our lives are not bound to the years we spend in our current bodies. Though this life is filled with blessings, it also has its share of trials. But one day we'll seamlessly leave this body and enter eternity, arriving at a place where God's presence is all the light we need and where there will be no more tears. John's reward—and ours—awaits.

Father, thank You for this reminder that good things await me in heaven. Give me strength to get through these current times.

COMPASSION

When he went ashore he saw a great crowd, and he had compassion on them, because they were like sheep without a shepherd. And he began to teach them many things.
MARK 6:34

It's easy to *say* we love all people. After all, we're Christians. Of course we love everyone in a generic, keep-your-distance kind of way. But deep down, we often look at the masses and think, *People are idiots.*

That attitude has zero resemblance to the way Christ viewed people. When He looked at the crowds clamoring for miracles, He had compassion. He was moved with love for them, for He knew they were helpless and needed a Savior.

We were helpless too. Like the people in the crowd that day, we were lost.

As Christ-followers, we're called to love like He loves. God wants us to look at the masses—at the dirty, the immoral, the foolish, the wicked, the vile—and have compassion. Those are people who need a Savior. It's our job to show them the way to the one who can meet their needs.

Father, I'm ashamed to say I'm not always the most compassionate person—especially with people I disagree with or who have offended me in some way. But they are like sheep without a shepherd. They're lost. They're vulnerable. And they need You. Show me how to relate to them. Help me to love like You love.

REACH FOR HIM

*And wherever he came, in villages, cities, or countryside,
they laid the sick in the marketplaces and implored him
that they might touch even the fringe of his garment.
And as many as touched it were made well.*

MARK 6:56

Jesus must have grown weary of all the crowds, of everyone wanting to touch Him and speak with Him. Though He was clearly comfortable in large groups, there is evidence He was an introvert. He often went away from the crowds to recharge, to pray, to spend time alone before reengaging with people. The thought of going to another town where people would clamor for a piece of Him must have been exhausting.

But He did it anyway. The reason? He *loved* people. He loved them *so much*, and He knew they were hurting. He knew they needed what only He could give. Nothing in this world could have kept Him away.

He loves us that way too. He cares about our illnesses, our heartaches, our financial troubles, and our relationships. He cares about everything we care about. And for every problem, He is still the solution. He still heals the sick or gives us strength to endure the affliction. He lifts up the hurting and makes us stronger for the experience.

What do you need from Jesus today? Reach for Him. Touch the fringe of His garment through prayer and the study of His Word. He is there for you.

You know what I need, what I'm going through right now, Lord. I'm reaching for You. I trust You completely.

ALL THINGS WELL

*And they were astonished beyond measure, saying,
"He has done all things well. He even makes
the deaf hear and the mute speak."*
MARK 7:37

Everywhere Jesus went, crowds followed. They wanted miracles. They wanted to hear what this man had to say. Even when He told them to keep what they heard and saw to themselves for now, they couldn't stay quiet. They had to tell everyone!

As with any celebrity, Jesus' every move was scrutinized. And what others saw was profound. "It's like He doesn't have any flaws! Everything He does, He does with excellence."

God hasn't called most of us to heal the sick or preach to crowds of thousands. But He has called us to be like Christ. We have a holy, reverent obligation to *do all things well.*

That doesn't mean we have to be good at everything. We have different gifts and talents and abilities. But each of us has the option of doing what we do half-heartedly or with all our hearts, "as working for the Lord" (Colossians 3:23 NIV). Driving a carpool? Do it with a sweet spirit and joy in your heart. Fixing dinner? Make it delicious, and serve it with a smile. Whether you're an accountant, a hair stylist, or a college professor, people are watching you. They know you belong to God. And your effort and attitude are a reflection on Him. Let them look at you and say, "She does all things well."

Lord, I want to honor You in all I do.

LAGOM

"For what does it profit a man to gain the whole world and forfeit his soul? For what can a man give in return for his soul?"
MARK 8:36–37

In Sweden, there's a term called *lagom*. It means "just right" or "just enough." Lagom is the concept of finding balance and practicing moderation instead of always striving for more. This principle seems to be lost in much of our modern society. We're bombarded through ads and social media and culture that more is better and that less is settling.

The lie here is that *more* means *happier*. The opposite is true. Research has shown that once our basic material needs for food, clothing, and shelter are met, happiness does not increase through money or things. They may offer a temporary smile or two, but grasping for more only leads to discontent.

This constant climb for more money, more success, and more prestige is making us miserable. We can gain the world yet lose our souls in the process. Paul, in his letter to the Philippians, talked about the importance of being content in any circumstance. Jesus said the same thing here, using different words. If anything is worth striving for, it's more of God. More of His presence. He will fill up our souls with His joy, His peace, and His love.

I'm sorry for focusing on the wrong things instead of seeking more of You, Father. I know You are the only one who can fill the longing in my heart.

HELP MY UNBELIEF

"But if you can do anything, have compassion on us and help us." And Jesus said to him, "'If you can'! All things are possible for one who believes." Immediately the father of the child cried out and said, "I believe; help my unbelief!"

MARK 9:22–24

This man came to Jesus with his son, who was mute. The boy also had seizures that caused him to fall to the ground and foam at the mouth. Some translations of the Bible say the boy had an unclean spirit. The father, desperate for his child, brought him to Christ. He had heard about all the people Jesus had healed.

But he said, "If You can, will You do this?"

Jesus replied, "What do you mean, 'If I can'? Haven't I done enough? When will you people believe that I am who I say I am?"

We often come to Christ the same way this father did. We say, "God, if You're able, please do this or that." Yet He longs to hear us say, "God, I *know* You can do this. You're the only one who can."

We're all on a journey of faith. Time and experience help us understand God's power. In the meantime, it's okay to say exactly what this man said: "I believe! Help my unbelief!"

> Father, I want my faith to be strong. I believe in Your power. I know You are God, and nothing is impossible for You. Whatever doubt is in my mind, please remove it. Help my unbelief!

SERVANT OF ALL

*And he sat down and called the twelve.
And he said to them, "If anyone would be first,
he must be last of all and servant of all."*
MARK 9:35

In this verse, the word *first* comes from a Greek root, *protos*. It means first in honor, first in rank, first in influence. Just before Jesus said this, His disciples had been arguing with each other about who was the greatest among them. When He asked what they were talking about, they remained silent. They probably recognized that Jesus wouldn't approve of such a discussion.

In their minds, the greatest would be served by the least. But God's way is the opposite. It goes against our human nature. God's way says the greatest among us is the one who serves others best. Jesus demonstrated this when He washed the disciples' feet—a job typically reserved for a low-ranking servant. And He demonstrated it once for all when He died in our place.

How can we become great? By serving others. By making sure others' needs are met. As we do so, we get out of our own heads and find that many of our anxieties shrink. As we do so, we practice humility, which pleases God. And as we do so, we show others what Christ's love really looks like.

Lord, I'm sorry for putting myself first and
for wanting to be important and recognized.
Teach me to serve others in a way that pleases You.

LIKE A CHILD

And they were bringing children to him that he might touch them, and the disciples rebuked them. But when Jesus saw it, he was indignant and said to them, "Let the children come to me; do not hinder them, for to such belongs the kingdom of God."

MARK 10:13–14

Have you ever noticed how easy it is for a small child to trust? Whatever is scary or unsettling is all better once he's in Mom's or Dad's arms. That's how God wants us to trust Him. But the older we get, and the more we see that people are flawed, the harder it is for us to trust. That's why Jesus said we need to be like children.

When life gets hard, don't be like an adult, trying to fix everything on your own. Be like a child who brings the problem to a parent to fix. Whether it's a broken toy, a broken dream, or a broken relationship, stand before God, arms up, and say, "I need You. I know You're the one who can make this right." That kind of simple trust capture's God's heart and opens the floodgate for His blessings.

There is so much brokenness in my life, Father—so many doors that only You can open and situations that only You can change. I'm sorry for trying to handle things on my own. I need Your help, and I trust You completely.

IS HE WORTH IT?

And Jesus, looking at him, loved him, and said to him, "You lack one thing: go, sell all that you have and give to the poor, and you will have treasure in heaven; and come, follow me." Disheartened by the saying, he went away sorrowful, for he had great possessions.

MARK 10:21–22

A rich young man asked Jesus what he needed to do to earn eternal life. He had lived a good life, following all the commandments in the Old Testament. But Jesus knew the man still didn't put God first. When He told this fellow to sell all his possessions and donate the proceeds to the poor, the young man went away sad. That was something he wasn't willing to do.

Technically, there's nothing wrong with being wealthy. God blesses us so we can bless others. But when we put money *or anything else* in front of God—when we say, "I can't do that. That's more important to me than pleasing God"—we forfeit the greatest blessing of all: our relationship with God.

We all get our priorities out of whack sometimes. The important thing is that we acknowledge it, ask God to change our hearts, and live in obedience to Him. He probably won't ask us to sell all our possessions. . .but whatever He asks, He is worth it.

Father, show me if I've placed anyone or anything ahead of my relationship with You. Help me rearrange my priorities. You are more important to me than anything.

WHY HE DID IT

And taking the twelve again, he began to tell them what was to happen to him, saying, "See, we are going up to Jerusalem, and the Son of Man will be delivered over to the chief priests and the scribes, and they will condemn him to death and deliver him over to the Gentiles. And they will mock him and spit on him, and flog him and kill him. And after three days he will rise."

MARK 10:32–34

Most of us, if we knew something horrible would happen to us, would run for the hills. Or we'd at least fight against it. We'd round up every ally we could find and encourage them to fight with us. But Christ didn't do that. He knew what was coming. And He walked into it willingly.

Why would He do such a thing? Why would any sane person calmly describe the worst imaginable outcome with such acceptance?

The reason is *love*. Jesus knew the punishment for sin was death. And though He had no sin of His own, He knew there was no way we could pay that price for ourselves. We'd just stay dead—an eternal death, separated from God. The only way for us to experience eternal life was if someone paid that price for us.

He died for us. Now He asks that we *live* for Him.

Thank You, Jesus, for giving Your life for me.
Though I could never repay Your gift, I want to
offer my life in exchange as I live each day for You.

WHAT FAITH CAN DO

And Jesus said to him, "What do you want me to do for you?" And the blind man said to him, "Rabbi, let me recover my sight." And Jesus said to him, "Go your way; your faith has made you well." And immediately he recovered his sight and followed him on the way.

MARK 10:51–52

Most of us know we're supposed to pray about things. When storms come, we're supposed to ask Him to help. But too often we only ask for things we think are reasonable. We figure out what we could make happen if circumstances were right. We come up with a plan, and we approach God with it. But God is so much bigger than that! He's not bound by our limited understanding of practical solutions.

The man in today's scripture passage could have asked for food or for a home. He could have asked for someone to take care of him. But he knew all these problems would be solved if only he weren't blind. He asked Christ for the best thing he could think of: his sight.

Are you limiting God with your prayers? Tell Him what you want. Tell Him the true desires of your heart, even if they seem impossible. Trust Him and see what happens. No matter the outcome, God will be pleased by your faith, and He will bless you.

I'm sorry if I've limited You in my mind, Father. You know what I face. You know the desires of my heart. You are the only one who can fulfill them. I trust You completely.

THE COLT

*[Jesus] said to them, "Go into the village opposite you,
and immediately as you enter it you will find a colt tied there,
on which no one has ever sat; untie it and bring it here."*
MARK 11:2 NASB

The incident in this passage takes place on what's often referred to as Palm Sunday. As Christ rode into Jerusalem on a colt, a big crowd welcomed Him. They shouted and swayed their arms and waved palm branches. Some might call it a parade.

Why would Jesus send His disciples to get a colt "on which no one has ever sat"? Colts need to be trained to carry a rider. In this setting especially, the colt would have been skittish. But though this one had never been ridden, it was just fine. The colt didn't need to be trained because animals obey their masters. God created the colt, and the colt submitted to Jesus.

Sometimes God calls us to do something we feel unprepared for. We look at God and say, "I can't. I've never done this before." But if God asks us to do something, He's just asking us to submit to Him. Obey Him. Trust Him. Follow His orders. Then give Him the glory for what He does.

---

*Sometimes I feel overwhelmed by what You ask me
to do, Father. Instead of doubting You, I want to be
like that colt. Help me trust You, obey You, and let
You work through me however You choose.*

GOOD FRUIT

On the next day, when they had left Bethany, He became hungry. Seeing from a distance a fig tree in leaf, He went to see if perhaps He would find anything on it; and when He came to it, He found nothing but leaves, for it was not the season for figs. And He said to it, "May no one ever eat fruit from you again!" And His disciples were listening.

MARK 11:12–14 NASB

This story has been the subject of much speculation. Why would Jesus curse a tree? Did He lose His temper? Was He so hungry He lost control?

To better understand what happened here, it helps to look at the Old Testament. Several times, Israelites are compared to a fig tree, especially when they're not producing good fruit (Jeremiah 8; Hosea 9; Micah 7). Israel's job was to show God to the world. Instead, God's people often turned away from Him and worshipped other gods. God told them if they didn't produce good fruit, they'd be cut off.

Jesus used this as an illustration. He's showing us that a true child of God can be identified by their fruit. Is a fig tree that doesn't produce figs *really* even a fig tree?

Is a "Christian" who doesn't display God's character *really* a Christian?

This is a hard passage, for sure, because none of us produces perfect fruit all the time. But if His Spirit lives in us, others will see evidence.

Lord, help me produce good fruit that points others to You.

HYPOCRITES

Some Sadducees (who say that there is no resurrection) came to Jesus, and began questioning Him, saying... "In the resurrection, which one's wife will she be? For each of the seven had her as his wife."
MARK 12:18, 23 NASB

A group of religious leaders asked Jesus a question. If a woman was married to several different men, and each one died before she married the next, who will she be married to in heaven? It's important to understand that the Sadducees didn't even believe in the resurrection. To them, it was a non-issue. They asked Jesus this question not out of a genuine desire to understand but from a plan to trick Him.

What hypocrisy.

Sometimes our human nature urges us into manipulation and trickery to prove a point or get our way. That is not of God. Our Lord wants us to be honest and straightforward in all our communication. This kind of authenticity pleases God and earns us respect from others.

Jesus saw through their plan and answered that in heaven, we'll be alive but changed. We won't marry. The Sadducees' deceit failed, and the people around most likely saw right through it. Trickery, manipulation, and lies are never from God, and they have no place in the life of a Christian.

I'm guilty of manipulating things to get my way. I'm sorry for that, Lord. Teach me to be honest and straightforward like You.

LOVE GOD, LOVE PEOPLE

> *"'And you shall love the Lord your God with all your heart, and with all your soul, and with all your mind, and with all your strength.' The second is this: 'You shall love your neighbor as yourself.' There is no other commandment greater than these."*
>
> MARK 12:30–31 NASB

The Old Testament is filled with rules and regulations people had to follow to stay right with God. Many of these guidelines were there for one purpose: to highlight the fact that we can't ever be good enough to earn our way to heaven. It's God's grace, not our works, that gives us the right to become children of God.

Yet the religious people clung to these rules. This form of legalism allowed them to separate people into "good" and "bad" categories based on how well they complied. They asked Jesus all kinds of questions to stump Him, but He always answered with wisdom. When they asked about the most important of God's laws, Jesus answered with these verses. In Matthew's version of this story, Jesus said, "This sums up the Law and the Prophets" (Matthew 7:12 NIV). In other words, everything in God's law and everything the prophets taught us hinge on these two commands.

Love God above all else. Love others and look out for them the way you look out for yourself. How can you live out these commands today?

I love You, Father, with all my heart, soul, and mind. Teach me to love others well.

REACHING THE WORLD

And the gospel must first be preached to all the nations.
MARK 13:10 NASB

As Jesus spoke to His disciples about the end times, some of them asked Him how they'd recognize that the time was upon them. The verse above, about preaching to all the nations, was part of His answer. Though we can't know when Christ will return, we do know His heart has always been to make sure everyone has a chance to choose Him. We are getting close! With the work of Bible translators coupled with the internet now available to 80 percent of the world, we can see how the time is soon. But it's not time yet.

What can we do to bring the gospel to all the nations? Donating money to and praying for missionaries and Bible translation ministries is one way. But there are people all around us who, despite having a church down the street, have never heard the gospel. Will you tell them?

Ask God to show you how He wants to use your gifts, your talents, and your personality to share His love. Invite the grocery cashier to church with you. Leave your waitress an extra-big tip, along with a note that God loves her and a Bible verse. Invite your coworker for coffee and share your story about how God has worked in your life. We can't all reach thousands. But if we all work together, God will use our efforts to reach the world.

**Father, show me what You want me to
do to reach the world with Your love.**

ROLL AWAY THE STONE

They were saying to one another, "Who will roll away the stone from the entrance of the tomb for us?" And looking up, they noticed that the stone had been rolled away; for it was extremely large.

MARK 16:3–4 NASB

After Jesus' death, a group of women went to His tomb with spices to anoint His body. They knew there was a big stone covering the tomb. They may not have been aware that it was guarded and that Pilate had put a wax seal on the stone to make sure it wasn't tampered with. But even the thought of moving the enormous stone must have had these ladies a little concerned.

But that's what faith looks like. God asks us to do something to honor Him, and we may not be exactly sure how it will get done. We may not feel qualified. We may have concerns. But we move forward anyway, out of love and obedience, trusting that God will take care of things at the right time.

What has God asked you to do? Take the first step in faith. Talk to Him about your concerns and let Him know you can't do it without Him. Then make the phone call or open your computer or apply for the job or do whatever He's prompted you to do. Keep moving forward, and watch the miracles unfold.

Father, I will obey You, but I don't know how it will play out. I trust You to roll away the stone.

HUMBLED

"But go, tell His disciples and Peter, 'He is going ahead of you to Galilee; there you will see Him, just as He told you.'"
MARK 16:7 NASB

Have you ever wondered why Jesus set Peter apart when He asked the women to spread the word? Most scholars believe it's because Peter had separated himself at this point. Remember, Peter had promised before the crucifixion that he would never deny Christ.

That's when Jesus looked at Peter and said, "You'll deny Me three times before the rooster crows tomorrow morning." Sure enough, that's exactly what happened. Peter, along with the other disciples, was afraid for his life. Most of them made themselves scarce during that time. But because Peter had made such a bold promise and then broken it, he was ashamed. He couldn't face his friends.

Peter, who had once been all bluster and bravado—recall that he was the only one to step out of the boat and walk on water (Matthew 14)—has now been humbled. It was to Peter that Jesus said, "On this rock I will build my church" (Matthew 16:18 ESV). Peter's name meant "rock," and yet Peter had failed to be a rock when it counted most.

Still, Jesus sought Peter out. Jesus knew beforehand about Peter's flaws, and He still wanted to use him. He knows about our weaknesses too. Sometimes our failures humble us, and God chooses to work through humble people.

I know You see all my failures, Lord. I'm not worthy, but I'm Yours to use however You want.

CHOSEN

*Now after He had risen early on the first day of
the week, He first appeared to Mary Magdalene,
from whom He had cast out seven demons.*

MARK 16:9 NASB

Seven demons? Wow. Here's a woman with a past. And yet Jesus chose her to be the first one He appeared to after His resurrection.

Satan often tries to keep us from reaching our full potential in Christ by reminding us of our past. Maybe we made poor choices that hurt other people. Maybe we lived through some kind of abuse or trauma, and we don't think we're worthy of living a joyful, peace-filled life. We cling to our past like dried, caked-on mud, and we forget that Christ has washed us clean.

We're clean of our own mistakes. We're also free of the hurts others have placed on us. As with Mary Magdalene, Christ singles us out for something special. Once we come to Him, once we accept all He's done for us on the cross, we're no longer the dirty, mud-caked people we once were. We are clean. We are loved. We are chosen.

Thank You for seeing the best version of me, Lord.
Forgive me for listening to Satan and for clinging to my past.
I know Satan is a liar. He wants to remind me of who I used to be,
but I'm no longer that person. Thank You for who I am in You.

PARTNERS

*And they went out and preached everywhere,
while the Lord worked with them, and confirmed
the word by the signs that followed.*
MARK 16:20 NASB

When someone is about to leave for a long time, whether because they are dying or because they are going on a long trip, they often leave their loved ones with some important words to remember. In this passage, Jesus had just ascended to heaven after His resurrection. He'd told His disciples to go into all the world and make more disciples, and He'd promised to stay with them always (Matthew 28:20).

The disciples did what Christ asked them to do, and Jesus kept up His end of the bargain. All they said and did was confirmed by signs from the Holy Spirit. The promise He gave them still holds true for us today. When we obey Him, when we do His work in faith, He comes alongside us. He doesn't leave us alone to accomplish things. Instead, He encourages us and those around us with signs, with open doors, with results that can only come from God.

Though our work for God can't always be measured by the world's ideas of success, we can gain confidence in knowing God sees our efforts and joins us in our work. And nothing is more fulfilling than knowing you've been hand-chosen to partner with the King of kings.

Thank You for choosing me to do Your work, Father, and for joining me. I can't do it alone—but I also know I don't have to.

HE NEVER FAILS

Zechariah said to the angel, "How will I know this? For I am an old man, and my wife is advanced in her years." The angel answered and said to him, "I am Gabriel, who stands in the presence of God, and I was sent to speak to you and to bring you this good news. And behold, you will be silent and unable to speak until the day when these things take place, because you did not believe my words, which will be fulfilled at their proper time."
LUKE 1:18–20 NASB

Zechariah and his wife were righteous and blameless. They had no children. So when the angel came to tell Zechariah that they'd give birth to a very special child, Zechariah responded by asking, "How can this be? We're too old!"

That fleeting moment of doubt caused God to discipline Zechariah. He'd be mute until the child was born. This may seem harsh, and it might have been for someone less experienced. But when we are at a place in our lives when we *should* trust God—when our maturity and life experience have taught us many times over about God's power and goodness—and instead of trusting, we doubt, there are consequences.

Our lives are a journey toward maturity in Christ. Has He ever failed you? Those of us who have known Him for some time can honestly, enthusiastically say, "No! He has never failed. Not even once."

Hold on to the maturity He's given you. Trust Him, and never doubt.

I trust You, Lord, even when things don't make sense.

MARY'S SONG

"For the Mighty One has done great things for me; and holy is His name. And His mercy is to generation after generation toward those who fear Him."
Luke 1:49–50 nasb

For most, being a pregnant, unwed teen mother wouldn't be a cause for rejoicing. . .at least not initially. Although she was innocent, Mary's circumstances brought gossip and speculation. Most people would have wondered, *Why me?* But Mary showed great spiritual maturity, even at her young age. She knew God had chosen her for something special, and she praised Him.

Next time things don't go your way, remember this passage from Luke 1. Remember Mary, who was young and afraid. Yet she set her own feelings aside to see the bigger picture. She knew that despite her current hardship, she would play an important role in God's overall plan.

What great things does God have in store for you? What bigger picture might God be working toward? How has He inserted you into that purpose? What role will you play in His plan? Whatever you face, try to sing Mary's song in the middle of it.

Father, You have done great things for me. Your name is holy. Your mercy flows from the generations before me to those beyond me—it never ends. Thank You for including me in Your plan. I praise You for what You're doing, and I'm grateful to be a part of it.

PEACE ON EARTH

"Glory to God in the highest, and on earth peace among people with whom He is pleased."
LUKE 2:14 NASB

Imagine being a shepherd in that moment. . .working the night shift, trying to stay awake, when an angel suddenly appears with a message from God. Then, as if that weren't enough, a whole bunch of angels show up singing, "Glory to God!" What a story.

These words are beautifully scripted across Christmas cards and above nativity scenes. Many focus on the "peace on earth" part, and rightfully so. God's peace is certainly a gift worth pursuing. But the rest of the phrase is important: "And on earth peace among people with whom He is pleased."

God's promises are for those who believe, who accept His Son, and who live to honor Him. Those are the ones God is pleased with. Hebrews 11:6 tells us that without *faith* it is impossible to please God.

How can you live out your faith today? How can you please God? Instead of worrying, trust Him. Instead of retaliating, leave it to God. Make it your goal, in all your actions and thoughts, to honor God. He doesn't demand perfection, but He is pleased with those who sincerely seek Him.

Thank You for Your promises, Father. I know they are given to those who believe and who live to please You. I'm Yours. All I have, all I am, is Yours. I want to honor You.

PONDER

But Mary treasured all these things, pondering them in her heart. And the shepherds went back, glorifying and praising God for all that they had heard and seen, just as had been told them.
LUKE 2:19–20 NASB

Imagine giving birth to your first child and having a bunch of smelly, sweaty shepherds show up! While most of us would be exhausted and annoyed, while most of us would want these strangers to leave us alone, Mary quietly watched. She absorbed everything that happened and pondered it in her heart.

To ponder means to think about or reflect on something. It means to consider something calmly, soberly, and deeply. God wants us to ponder Him.

Do we think about God all the time? Do we watch the events of our lives with expectation, wondering how God will put them all together to bring glory to Himself and to point people to His goodness? Do we glorify and praise God for all we've seen and heard, because we know God is at work?

God has allowed us to play a part in His epic story. Don't miss it! Like Mary, watch and ponder. Like the shepherds, glorify and praise God for how He's moving. These intentional acts will transform our hearts, and we'll be filled with joy and awe.

Lord, sometimes I let things slip by unnoticed, without pondering how You're working. Teach me to slow down, be present, and take note of the wonderful things You're doing.

ANNA

And there was a prophetess, Anna, the daughter of Phanuel, of the tribe of Asher. She was advanced in years and had lived with her husband for seven years after her marriage, and then as a widow to the age of eighty-four. She did not leave the temple grounds, serving night and day with fasts and prayers. And at that very moment she came up and began giving thanks to God, and continued to speak about Him to all those who were looking forward to the redemption of Jerusalem.
LUKE 2:36–38 NASB

There is so much to unpack in these three verses. First, Anna was a prophetess. In a culture where women were often dismissed, the writer (and others) recognized that God's hand was on this woman's life. From the time of her husband's death when she was still young, she had spent every possible moment at the temple, praying and fasting and worshipping God.

God rewarded her faithfulness by letting her see Jesus in person! She was one of the first to let everyone know that this child was the promised Messiah.

How is God waiting to bless you today? We never know what's in store when we simply live faithful, quiet lives, honoring God and showing up for Him every day.

Father, I want to be consistent and faithful like Anna. Even if no one else notices, I know You see me. Thank You for the blessings You have in store for me every day.

LIKE CHRIST

Now the Child continued to grow and to become strong, increasing in wisdom; and the favor of God was upon Him.
LUKE 2:40 NASB

This verse was written about Christ, the Son of God. But ideally, it could be written about any of us. Even as adults, we should never stop growing, becoming strong, or increasing in wisdom. When we live our lives to please God, His favor rests on us.

How do we grow in Christ? The most straightforward way is to read His Word. Hebrews 4:12 tells us His Word is alive and active. By filling our minds with it every day, we take in spiritual nourishment. We ingest godly vitamins and minerals that help us grow more like Him.

How do we become strong in Him? In addition to reading His Word, we build spiritual muscle by working out. Just as working out our bodies makes us physically stronger, exercising our faith makes us spiritually stronger. When we're tempted to worry or become anxious, we choose to trust the Lord instead. When we're upset or annoyed, we choose to act with love. When we practice our faith, we become stronger.

How do we become wise? James 1:5 tells us to ask God. He is the source of wisdom, and He won't hold back from anyone who sincerely asks. When we grow, become strong, and increase in wisdom, we become like Christ, and we find God's favor.

**Like Christ, I never want to stop growing.
I want to be strong and wise in You, Lord God.**

BE GENEROUS

*John replied, "If you have two shirts, give one to the poor.
If you have food, share it with those who are hungry."*
LUKE 3:11 NLT

Culture tells us that we need more. No matter how much we have, it never feels like enough. And not just our society, but it seems every society—from the beginning of time—has valued riches and wealth. But God's way is different from our way, and His way is always best. Instead of seeking more, we discover there's great value in knowing what's *enough*. Too much stuff causes stress, because we just must organize it and clean it, box it and store it. How much better to keep only what we need and bless others with our excess? Instead of gathering dust, that expensive too-small dress can benefit someone else who needs it but can't afford it. Instead of taking up space, that extra set of dishes can be used by a struggling family.

God doesn't bless us so we can hoard. He gives us more than we need so we can bless others and be His hands and feet here on earth. What do you have in your closet or your garage or even your bank account that others could use? Be generous with others and God will continue to be generous with you.

**I'm sorry for holding on to things I don't need
when others could use them, Lord. Teach me
to be generous with Your blessings.**

WHAT A LIAR!

Then the devil took him up and revealed to him all the kingdoms of the world in a moment of time. "I will give you the glory of these kingdoms and authority over them," the devil said, "because they are mine to give to anyone I please. I will give it all to you if you will worship me."
LUKE 4:5–7 NLT

It took a lot of nerve for Satan to look right into Jesus' eyes and lie. But because Satan is shameless, that's exactly what he did. Satan is a liar. If Jesus had given in and worshipped him, Satan would not have delivered on his promise anyway. Or he'd have delivered on it, and the price would have been too high and Jesus would have been miserable.

What things does Satan promise you? What does he tempt you with? Remember, he's a liar, and his goal isn't to bring you joy. More than anything, he wants to *steal* your joy. He promises wealth, but often at the cost of our families. He promises happiness, but he doesn't tell us it's short-lived. Be like Jesus in Luke 4:8 and quote scripture to the devil. Tell him to get lost, and then cling to God's promises. God always, *always* delivers.

I'm sorry for getting drawn in by Satan's lies, Lord.
He's hurt me so many times, and I should know better.
Thank You for the wisdom that comes with experience.
Next time I start to fall for one of Satan's schemes,
remind me of Your promises and pull me back to You.

THE FOLLY OF PEOPLE PLEASING

"The Spirit of the Lord is upon me, for he has anointed me to bring Good News to the poor. He has sent me to proclaim that captives will be released, that the blind will see, that the oppressed will be set free, and that the time of the Lord's favor has come."... When they heard this, the people in the synagogue were furious. Jumping up, they mobbed him and forced him to the edge of the hill on which the town was built. They intended to push him over the cliff.
Luke 4:18–19, 28–29 NLT

Why were these people so angry? Jesus was speaking God's truth, not hurting anyone. Yet they were jealous. After all, He was one of them. They knew His parents. They said, "Isn't this that kid from Galilee? You know...that carpenter's son. Who does He think He is?" They didn't like the idea that one of their own would surpass them in greatness.

Jesus didn't argue with them. In fact, He didn't respond at all. He just slipped away. Moved on to another place where He could continue His calling. When you're doing what you know God has called you to do and others discourage you, move on. Be polite. Pray for them. Let your actions—and the results—speak for themselves. Remember, you answer to God, not anyone else.

Heavenly Father, sometimes I'm too much of a people-pleaser. Remind me to be a God-pleaser. Your opinion of me is the only one that matters.

MANIPULATION

On another Sabbath day, a man with a deformed right hand was in the synagogue while Jesus was teaching. The teachers of religious law and the Pharisees watched Jesus closely. If he healed the man's hand, they planned to accuse him of working on the Sabbath.... At this, the enemies of Jesus were wild with rage and began to discuss what to do with him.

LUKE 6:6–7,11 NLT

Gossip. Slander. Manipulation. This reads like a bad soap opera. Let's take Jesus out of the story for just a minute. Is it ever okay to try to trap someone? Is manipulation ever the best option? Is it good and holy and right to whisper and plan someone's demise?

Gossip and slander have been called the "Christian" sins of choice. We stand firm behind the high-profile, newsworthy issues while destroying each other with our words. We make plans to catch people breaking our rules so we can humiliate them. These men didn't care about the man's hand. They only cared about bringing Jesus down. This is why so many have turned away from the church. We act more like the religious people in the passage above than like God.

Remember, God is love. His actions are always and only driven by love. Next time you feel yourself trying to manipulate a situation, ask God to fill your heart with love and push out everything else.

**I don't want to be like the Pharisees, Father.
Instead, I want to be like Christ, always acting in love.**

WHEN IT DOESN'T MAKE SENSE

When he had finished speaking, he said to Simon, "Now go out where it is deeper, and let down your nets to catch some fish." "Master," Simon replied, "we worked hard all last night and didn't catch a thing. But if you say so, I'll let the nets down again." And this time their nets were so full of fish they began to tear!
LUKE 5:4–6 NLT

Have you ever felt God nudging you to do something that didn't make sense? That's how Simon felt. They'd fished all night and caught nothing. Now Jesus was telling them to lower their nets?

Jesus knew what Simon didn't. Because Simon obeyed, even when he didn't see the point, he was blessed. God will never lead us to do something that goes against His Word or His character. But when you feel He's leading you to act in a way that's consistent with His purpose, trust Him. Even if it seems crazy, act in faith. He may fill your net with fish. He may lead someone into your path who needs friendship. You may never know His purpose or see results, but trust Him anyway. Our faith pleases Him and leads to His blessings.

> Sometimes I know You're telling me to do something, but it doesn't make sense, Lord. So I talk myself out of it, or I let others discourage me. I'm sorry for not trusting You. Teach me to obey You even when I don't understand. More than anything, I want to please You.

SELF-CARE

*But despite Jesus' instructions, the report of his power
spread even faster, and vast crowds came to hear him
preach and to be healed of their diseases. But Jesus
often withdrew to the wilderness for prayer.*

Luke 5:15–16 nlt

Jesus' main purpose for leaving His throne in heaven and coming to earth was to love us. He did that by meeting people, talking to them, healing them, and caring for their needs. You'd think He'd take advantage of every moment to do what He came to do. Yet He withdrew to the wilderness for prayer.

Didn't He pray without ceasing? Wasn't God with Him every moment? Why did He need to spend time alone?

While He was here, Christ inhabited a human body. He knew His limitations, and He needed that one-on-one time with His Father to recharge. He needed time to rest. To relax. To breathe. His withdrawal in this passage is what we might call "self-care."

If we're going to love others, we must love ourselves (Mark 12:31). This doesn't mean putting ourselves before others. It means taking care of our bodies, which are God's temple. It means making time alone with God a priority. It means doing whatever we need to do so we can be at our best for others.

Are you worn out? Do you feel like everyone's tugging at you? It's okay to withdraw. It's necessary to recharge. It's biblical!

Thank You, Father, for this reminder that I need to take care of my mind, body, and spirit. When I'm at my best, I can better love others.

THROUGH THE ROOF

Some men came carrying a paralyzed man on a sleeping mat. They tried to take him inside to Jesus, but they couldn't reach him because of the crowd. So they went up to the roof and took off some tiles. Then they lowered the sick man on his mat down into the crowd, right in front of Jesus. Seeing their faith, Jesus said to the man, "Young man, your sins are forgiven."
LUKE 5:18–20 NLT

Wouldn't you have loved to be on the scene when this happened? What a spectacle these men must have created. If I were the homeowner, I'd have been pretty upset when these guys tore up my roof! Yet Jesus saw their desperate desire to see their friend healed. They were acting in a combination of faith and love—two of God's favorite attributes.

People in the crowd must have thought these fellows were crazy. Some might have even been angry. After all, if this man and his friends had wanted to see Jesus, they should have gotten there early enough to get a good seat. But Jesus doesn't see things the way humans do. He knows what's going on in our hearts. He knows our most intimate fears and anxieties. He sees our courage, our doubts, and even our disobedience. He rewards those who respond to life's trials with faith, even when faith is hard.

You know what I'm facing now, Lord. Faith is hard. . .but I'm willing to climb on the roof like these men did. I trust You even when it's hard.

HIS POWER

Everyone tried to touch him, because healing power went out from him, and he healed everyone.
Luke 6:19 nlt

Can you imagine being in the same town with Jesus and hearing He had power to heal diseases? All you had to do was touch Him, and you'd be well. This is a mystery we may never fully understand until we get to heaven. Yet God's Word tells us in Mark 16 and John 14 that we as Christians have this same power. Jesus even said we'd do greater things than He did, as long as we have faith.

That's hard to wrap our minds around. Our faith isn't a magic bullet that causes God to respond to our every whim. Sometimes His plans are different than ours, and we don't always understand the greater purpose in suffering. Sometimes God heals cancer and other diseases here on earth. . .and sometimes He heals in heaven.

That doesn't change the power of faith. When you or someone you know has a need, ask Him. Believe in His power, and trust the outcome. Faith still moves mountains. And God never, ever fails.

Father, this kind of faith is hard, especially when I'm surrounded by skeptics. Yet I know You're the solution to every problem, the fulfillment of every need. I know that You are love and that You long to bless Your children. You know the mountain I'd like moved, Lord, and I trust You with the outcome. I need You to show Your power, Lord. You're the only one who can.

WHAT OTHERS THINK

When the Pharisee who had invited him saw this, he said to himself, "If this man were a prophet, he would know what kind of woman is touching him. She's a sinner!"... And Jesus said to the woman, "Your faith has saved you; go in peace."

LUKE 7:39, 50 NLT

It's human nature to care about what others think. Some of us dress to impress. Others seek higher education or better jobs. Or maybe we rely on our personality and charm to make others like us. In this scene, Jesus is eating dinner at a high-profile Pharisee's house. If He could get the Pharisees on His side, He'd be able to reach a lot more people!

So when this woman of questionable character came in and made a scene—crying at Jesus' feet, wetting His feet with her tears, then wiping them dry with her hair—it would have been easy for Jesus to say, "Not now, lady. Can't you see I'm in the middle of something?"

But Jesus is always more concerned with meeting our needs than with making a good impression, and that should be our approach too. Who do you know who needs your friendship? Even if they don't meet the standards of those around you, treat them with kindness. Look at them the way God does, as someone made in His image and who needs love.

Heavenly Father, help me care more about loving people than impressing them.

STORM CALMER

The disciples went and woke him up, shouting, "Master, Master, we're going to drown!" When Jesus woke up, he rebuked the wind and the raging waves. Suddenly the storm stopped and all was calm. Then he asked them, "Where is your faith?" The disciples were terrified and amazed. "Who is this man?" they asked each other. "When he gives a command, even the wind and waves obey him!"

LUKE 8:24–25 NLT

Studies have shown anxiety has increased 25 percent in recent years. In a world that seems so unstable, where wars and natural disasters and political discord and riots and school shootings have become commonplace, it's no wonder. Any one of us could be in that boat yelling, "Master! We're going to drown!"

But the same God who commands the winds and seas also commands world events. Proverbs 21:1 tells us He directs the hearts of kings. Though Jesus reprimanded His disciples for their lack of faith in that moment, He also calmed the storm. They were afraid, but they went to the right person, and it paid off.

God knows we're human. He knows we'll be afraid sometimes. But like the disciples, we can go to the one who holds all power. As we call out to Him, He may calm our storms. . .or He may calm our hearts. Either way, we can trust Him to take care of us.

Master, You see the storm surrounding me. Please don't let me drown.

WHAT MATTERS MOST

And he sent them out to proclaim the kingdom of God and to heal. And he said to them, "Take nothing for your journey, no staff, nor bag, nor bread, nor money; and do not have two tunics. And whatever house you enter, stay there, and from there depart."

LUKE 9:2–4

Looking forward, a year seems like a long time. Ten or twenty years can feel like an eternity. But when we look backward on the same amount of time, we realize how quickly the years slip by. Don't waste time worrying about things that won't matter in a decade. Trust God to provide those things!

Our main purpose, for the short time we're here, is to love God, love others, and help as many people as we can to understand His love. We've been sent here on a mission, and God will give us what we need for each day. We'll have riches aplenty in heaven. At that point, we won't have the opportunity for a do-over. If we spend all our energy here acquiring things that won't last and ignore our true calling, we'll throw away our chance for something greater—the chance to hear God say, "Well done."

Lord, I know it's easy to get distracted with wanting more. Help me to be satisfied with just enough while trusting You to meet all my future needs. Remind me to stay focused on my calling—to love You with all my heart and to love others the way You do.

WHO IS CHRIST?

Now it happened that as he was praying alone, the disciples were with him. And he asked them, "Who do the crowds say that I am?" And they answered, "John the Baptist. But others say, Elijah, and others, that one of the prophets of old has risen." Then he said to them, "But who do you say that I am?" And Peter answered, "The Christ of God."

LUKE 9:18–20

Jesus put His disciples on the spot when He asked, "Who do you say that I am?" He might as well be sitting with each of us reading this book, looking us in the eye and asking the same question.

Who do you say that I am?

If Christ is who we say He is, why do we worry? Why does anxiety keep us awake at night? What is the worst that could happen with Christ on our side? He is our Brother, our Father, our Savior, our King, and our Friend. He gave His life for us. Is anything impossible for Him?

What is on your mind today? What concern weighs heavy on your heart? Think of that thing. . .then hear Christ's voice asking that question. What is your answer? Can you trust Him?

I'm sorry I forget who You are sometimes, Lord. I know You are more than capable of handling all my concerns, and I know You're actively working on my behalf because You love me. Thank You for being my Savior and my Friend.

THE UNSUNG HEROES

After this the Lord appointed seventy-two others and sent them on ahead of him, two by two, into every town and place where he himself was about to go. And he said to them, "The harvest is plentiful, but the laborers are few. Therefore pray earnestly to the Lord of the harvest to send out laborers into his harvest."

LUKE 10:1–2

We hear a lot about Jesus' twelve disciples. But what about these seventy-two? They are some of the unsung heroes of the faith. There was a need, and they stepped up. They were chosen, and they accepted the call.

As followers of Christ, each one of us has been chosen. Will we be part of this seventy-two, or will we be like the massive crowds who followed Jesus when it was convenient but found excuses when things got hard? What an honor to have been called. What will our answer be?

There are so many in this world who don't know You, Lord. I often think about people on the other side of the globe, but there are people right across the street who need You. There are people in my office, in the stores and restaurants I go to, and all around my community. My answer is yes, Lord. I will answer the call. Show me where to go and what to say. I'm Yours to use as You want.

THE BETTER WAY

But Martha was distracted with much serving. And she went up to him and said, "Lord, do you not care that my sister has left me to serve alone? Tell her then to help me." But the Lord answered her, "Martha, Martha, you are anxious and troubled about many things, but one thing is necessary. Mary has chosen the good portion, which will not be taken away from her."
LUKE 10:40–42

Our society, perhaps more than at any other time in history, is filled with distractions. We have so many things to do, people to see, social media posts to like and share. . . When we're anxious or troubled, often our response is busyness. Instead of dealing with the source of our angst, we find things to do so we don't have to think about our problems. We try to control things by our actions.

But in those times, the *Mary* response is the best response. Slow down. Sit at Christ's feet like you're doing right now. Spend time with Him. Talk to Him and listen for His response. Grab a hymnal and sing to Him—He loves your voice. Or paint or write or worship Him in whatever way feels authentic and helps you relax in His presence.

Rest in Him. Soak Him in. This is the better way.

I've stayed so busy for so long that I've forgotten how to rest. Remind me, Lord. Teach me to be a Mary in a Martha world.

WHAT TO SAY

"And when they bring you before the synagogues and the rulers and the authorities, do not be anxious about how you should defend yourself or what you should say, for the Holy Spirit will teach you in that very hour what you ought to say."
LUKE 12:11–12

Anyone who's ever been slandered or lied about, anyone who's been the target of malicious gossip, knows how devastating it is to be falsely accused. Jesus warned us this would happen—Christians who live out their faith often make others uncomfortable and become targets. But He said, "Don't worry. I'll give you the words to say at the right time."

This is true for other situations as well. Maybe you want to share your faith with your neighbor but you don't know what to say. God will provide an opportunity so you don't have to force it, and He'll give you the words to say. Or maybe you're interviewing for a job or talking to your child's teacher, but you're nervous. Ask God to help you. Fill up on His wisdom, and it will come back to you in just the right moments. Rely on Him, and He will never leave you tongue-tied.

Father, You know how I struggle with words. I know what I want to say in my head, but it doesn't come out right. When I face enemies, I get anxious and freeze up. Make me bold with Your words and Your wisdom. I trust You to speak when I don't know what to say.

SETTLING UP

"As you go with your accuser before the magistrate, make an effort to settle with him on the way, lest he drag you to the judge, and the judge hand you over to the officer, and the officer put you in prison. I tell you, you will never get out until you have paid the very last penny."

Luke 12:58–59

God's Word talks a lot about peace. Whether it's embracing God's peace or living in peace with your neighbor, peace is a major theme of the Bible. It must be pretty important to God. Romans 12:18 tells us that as much as we're able, as much as it depends on us, we need to live at peace with others. This verse supports that sentiment. If you can settle something without calling in lawyers and judges, do it.

But there's a deeper meaning here as well. Satan is our accuser (Revelation 12:10). We owe him a debt—our lives! We are sinners, and Romans 6:23 says our wages (what we've earned) for sin is death. Satan wants to collect on that debt—eternal separation from God. Settle that debt now by accepting Christ—He paid it for you. If you wait too long and stand before the judge with the debt unsettled, it may be too late.

Help me to live at peace with everyone, Lord. I want to settle all my debts, especially the most important one. I accept Your gift of paying my debt on the cross. From now on, I belong to You.

THE RULES

But the ruler of the synagogue, indignant because Jesus had healed on the Sabbath, said to the people, "There are six days in which work ought to be done. Come on those days and be healed, and not on the Sabbath day." Then the Lord answered him, "You hypocrites! Does not each of you on the Sabbath untie his ox or his donkey from the manger and lead it away to water it? And ought not this woman, a daughter of Abraham whom Satan bound for eighteen years, be loosed from this bond on the Sabbath day?"
Luke 13:14–16

God gave His people rules to keep order. He wanted His people to take one day a week to rest and worship Him. But love is always at the heart of God's laws, not judgment. Jesus broke the rules and healed someone on the Sabbath because of love.

Legalism has no place in Christianity. Yes, rules are important, because they keep order. But the most important "rule" is believing that Christ is God's Son. Breaking this rule by denying Jesus' divinity will separate us from God. As for the rest of it. . .God wants us to honor Him and His laws, but He wants us to prioritize the most important ones: Love God with all your heart, and love others as you love yourself (Mark 12:30–31).

Lord, I'm sorry for the times I love the rules more than I love people. Teach me to love like You do.

THE CONTRAST

"If anyone comes to me and does not hate his own father and mother and wife and children and brothers and sisters, yes, and even his own life, he cannot be my disciple."

LUKE 14:26

Have you ever spent time at the beach and gotten a dark suntan? Someone may have commented about how white your teeth looked. Your teeth may have been the same color, but the *contrast* made them look whiter.

In this passage, Jesus is using hyperbole, a literary device that uses exaggeration to provide a contrast. God is all about love. He doesn't want us to hate anybody. But our love for God should be so big, so complete, so all-consuming that when we compare our love for others, it seems like hate. It's all about contrast.

The irony here is that the more we love God and the more He consumes us, the more our *love for others* will grow. Still, if anyone asks us to give up Christ for them or to deny God or to turn our back on our faith to prove our love, there should be no question. Our love for Christ trumps all.

I know You don't really want me to hate anyone, Father. Instead, You want my love and loyalty to You to be so great that nothing else compares. I want to love You more and more and more. . . . I want You to fill my every thought and breath and word. I know that the more I love You, the better I'll love those around me.

SALTY

"Salt is good, but if salt has lost its taste, how shall its saltiness be restored? It is of no use either for the soil or for the manure pile. It is thrown away. He who has ears to hear, let him hear."
LUKE 14:34–35

Most of us have a container of salt in the pantry or maybe sitting on the back of the stove. It's inexpensive, and it's one of the easiest ways to add flavor to food. But in Jesus' day, salt was used for a lot more than just seasoning the burgers. It preserved food. It was a healing compound. It was used as currency, to trade for other things. Jesus' listeners lived near the Dead Sea, which was filled with salt. They knew the importance of salt staying salty.

If salt gets wet, its properties are diluted. Once it has been diluted and then dried, the salt still looks the same—but it is *not* the same. The flavor's gone. Jesus compares our faith to salt. If we're Christians, our faith is our currency. It makes our lives savory. It heals our spirits. But sin dilutes our faith.

It's important to guard our hearts against sin, because the more we let sin into our lives, the weaker our faith becomes.

I want my faith to be strong, Lord. I'm sorry for the choices I make that dilute my faith. I want to stay close to You and keep my life free from sin. I don't want to lose my saltiness.

MONEY AND FAITH

And Zacchaeus stood and said to the Lord, "Behold, Lord, the half of my goods I give to the poor. And if I have defrauded anyone of anything, I restore it fourfold." And Jesus said to him, "Today salvation has come to this house, since he also is a son of Abraham."
LUKE 19:8–9

Zacchaeus was a tax collector. Tax collectors were known to be liars and cheaters, greedy for money. It was common for tax collectors to overcharge and pocket the extra cash. No one liked tax collectors. So when Jesus decided to have dinner with Zacchaeus, people wondered why on earth He would waste His time. But Zacchaeus' heart was ripe. He wanted to make his life right with God.

Matthew 6:21 tells us that where our treasure is, that's where our heart will be. Zacchaeus showed God He was most important by using his money in a way that honored Him—and by using it to make amends with others. If God were to look at your bank account, what would He find? Is your treasure spent on your own pleasure, or do you use what God gives you to please Him?

There's nothing wrong with spending your money for pleasure if that's not *all* you're using it for. When we find joy in giving, in helping, in serving God, He often blesses us with the other things we want as well.

Like Zacchaeus, I want to use my money to help others, to make things right as needed, and to honor You, Lord.

THE HAVES AND THE HAVE-NOTS

"I tell you that to everyone who has, more will be given, but from the one who has not, even what he has will be taken away."
LUKE 19:26

At first glance, this verse may seem harsh. Why would Jesus give more to the rich and take away from the poor? But this verse isn't just about money. Jesus is referring to anything God has given us. It might be material wealth or athletic ability or creativity. It might be the talent to make others laugh or the skill to organize anything from a vacation Bible school to a Fortune 500 company. Whatever gifts you have are from God. He trusted you with them so you could lead others to Him.

When we use what He has given us to please Him, He increases our reach, our influence, and our blessings. But when we do nothing with what He's given us, or we don't use it the way He intended, He'll take it away. We may lose our ability, or we may lose opportunities to use a specific talent.

What gifts, talents, and abilities has God given you? Are you using them for Him?

I don't feel like I have much to offer, Lord. But everything I have is Yours. Take it, use it, multiply it, and do with it whatever You want. I am Yours to spend in any way You see fit.

WISDOM

But he perceived their craftiness, and said to them, "Show me a denarius. Whose likeness and inscription does it have?" They said, "Caesar's." He said to them, "Then render to Caesar the things that are Caesar's, and to God the things that are God's."

LUKE 20:23–25

We can only imagine how intelligent Jesus must have been. After all, He was God's Son! But even more important than His intelligence was His wisdom. Both words are used to describe people who know a lot and who are quick thinking. But while intelligence refers to someone's ability to think logically about academic subjects, wisdom is all about practical life skills. You might think of intelligence as a college degree, while wisdom is street smarts. Jesus had both.

While we may be limited by our intelligence, there are no limits to the amount of wisdom we can obtain. James 1:5 tells us God will freely give wisdom to anyone who asks if He knows we're sincere and we'll really use it. Jesus got Himself out of a trap by using wisdom. Next time you're not sure what to do, ask God to make you wise. Then be humble enough to do what He says.

Sometimes I feel like I'm not very quick on my feet. I say or do the wrong thing at the wrong time. I need Your wisdom. When I face situations I'm unsure about, pour out Your wisdom. I know I can always count on You.

HUMILITY

While all the people were listening, Jesus said to his disciples, "Beware of the teachers of the law. They like to walk around in flowing robes and love to be greeted with respect in the marketplaces and have the most important seats in the synagogues and the places of honor at banquets. They devour widows' houses and for a show make lengthy prayers. These men will be punished most severely."
Luke 20:45–47 NIV

Jesus has no time for self-important people. We all know people like this—who want to be noticed, who buy the most expensive cars and have the most impressive houses, who want all the praise and all the accolades—and they'll do just about anything for attention. They care little about doing God's work. They just want to *look* like they're doing God's work so that others will think well of them.

The truth is, we all have a little bit of self-importance in us. It's part of our human nature. But God's way goes *against* our nature. He calls us to humility. He wants us to do His work without worrying about what others think. A humble person doesn't care about getting the credit as much as getting things done. While there's nothing wrong with wearing quality clothes or having nice things, the humble person doesn't make a show of it. Instead, they step quietly aside and point all attention, all praise and glory, to God.

Teach me to be humble, Lord. I want all the attention on You.

WHERE SHOULD I GO?

He replied, "As you enter the city, a man carrying a jar of water will meet you. Follow him to the house that he enters, and say to the owner of the house, 'The Teacher asks: Where is the guest room, where I may eat the Passover with my disciples?' He will show you a large room upstairs, all furnished. Make preparations there." They left and found things just as Jesus had told them. So they prepared the Passover.
LUKE 22:10–13 NIV

Do you ever worry about the future? If so, you're not alone. It's hard to be human and not be concerned about what tomorrow will bring. But Jesus already knows what's in store. He's already set everything in place to give you all you need.

At the time of these verses, a lot of important people wanted Jesus dead. It was also time for the Passover celebration, so Jesus asked Peter and John to go and get the meal ready. They asked, "Where should we go?" As you can see in today's passage, the Lord had everything under control.

Next time you wonder where you should go or what you should do, ask God. Then wait for His answer. Stay right where you are until He tells you to move. Trust Him. He has everything under control.

You know what I'm facing, Lord. You know all that concerns me. Tell me where to go and what to do. I trust You with the outcome.

MOCKED

*Then Herod and his soldiers ridiculed and mocked him.
Dressing him in an elegant robe, they sent him back to Pilate.*
Luke 23:11 niv

Few things are more humiliating than being mocked. Jesus, who'd done nothing but love people, heal the sick, feed the hungry, and spread the good news that God loved them, was publicly mocked. It's heartbreaking.

Jesus isn't the only one in the Bible to endure this kind of treatment. Job was mocked by his closest friends. King David was mocked by those who wanted to overthrow him. God has plenty to say about mockers—the bottom line is that He hates when people act this way, whether they mock Him or His children. Proverbs 3:34 tells us God mocks the mockers, but He gives grace to the humble.

The next time you feel mocked, teased, or bullied, remember that you're in good company! God sees. He cares. And He will take care of you. He will give you both strength and wisdom to stand up for yourself and others and to do it in a way that allows you to keep your cool and remain godly.

I feel so humiliated, Lord. Others are talking about me, making fun of me behind my back and to my face. I want to defend myself, but I don't know if it would do any good. Please make the bullying stop. Show me how to respond with strength, wisdom, and dignity. I need You to be my defender.

THE MOB

For the third time he spoke to them: "Why? What crime has this man committed? I have found in him no grounds for the death penalty. Therefore I will have him punished and then release him." But with loud shouts they insistently demanded that he be crucified, and their shouts prevailed. So Pilate decided to grant their demand. He released the man who had been thrown into prison for insurrection and murder, the one they asked for, and surrendered Jesus to their will.

LUKE 23:22–25 NIV

It's hard to understand how someone like Jesus—whom even Pilate knew was innocent—could be crucified. How did so many people—the same people who'd followed Him and hung on to His words—do such a quick turnabout?

These verses show us how. They had a mob mentality. And as awful as it is, it still happens today. Individually, we can tell right from wrong. But when enough people start pushing for something, it's easy to get swept up in the mood and go along with the crowd. After all, so many people can't be wrong, can they?

Yes, they can.

In a world where mob mentalities are the norm—whether in riots or cancel culture—be the difference. Sometimes it takes just one voice of reason to wake up a few people to what's happening. Then a few more take a stand. Even if your voice doesn't change the outcome, it will make an impression. Let others see Christ's light in you, even if you're the only one.

Heavenly Father, help me to stand up for what's right even when others don't.

PLACE OF HONOR

As the soldiers led him away, they seized Simon from Cyrene, who was on his way in from the country, and put the cross on him and made him carry it behind Jesus.
LUKE 23:26 NIV

Simon from Cyrene was just a bystander. He wasn't part of the mob that wanted Jesus killed. He was just passing through, minding his own business, when he ended up at the wrong place at the wrong time. Yet he was exactly where God wanted him to be.

He must have been a big man, a strong man. After being whipped and beaten, Jesus was made to carry His own cross. He collapsed under the weight. We don't know how much it weighed, but it was solid wood, so it would have been heavy. The soldiers pulled Simon from the crowd and made him carry it the rest of the way.

Carrying the cross was a punishment. Simon had done nothing to deserve that. It wasn't fair. Yet that act gave Simon the Cyrene a role in the greatest story ever told. It gave him a place of honor in God's Word.

What unfair hardship do you face? Hang in there. If you let Him, God will use this situation to give you a place of honor in His kingdom. One day, when He says, "Well done," you'll understand. You may even be grateful for what you endured.

You know what I'm facing, Father. It all feels so unfair. Yet even in this, I trust You.

UNDERESTIMATED

It was Mary Magdalene, Joanna, Mary the mother of James, and the others with them who told this to the apostles. But they did not believe the women, because their words seemed to them like nonsense.
LUKE 24:10–11 NIV

Throughout the ages and even today, women have been underestimated. Dismissed. Ignored. So the fact that the apostles didn't believe them isn't surprising. After all, everyone had watched Jesus die, and now these women said He was alive? We can imagine the eyes rolling.

But Jesus didn't underestimate His daughters. In fact, in a time and place where women had few rights, God's Word treated women with respect. In the Old Testament, the daughters of Zelophehad were given the rights of sons (Numbers 27:1–7; 36:2). Deborah was a judge (Judges 4). Anna was a prophetess (Luke 2:36–38). It's no surprise the women in today's passage were the first to see Jesus after His resurrection and were given the task of spreading the word.

We've all felt dismissed and underestimated at times. But God never underestimates His children! In fact, He empowers us to do all we've been called to do. Hold your head high, knowing you are a strong, capable daughter of the King.

Sometimes I place too much stock in what others think of me, Lord. I know I should only be concerned with what You think. Remind me of who I am in You and give me strength, wisdom, and dignity to accomplish Your purpose for me.

GOD'S LIVING WORD

In the beginning was the Word, and the Word was with God, and the Word was God. He was with God in the beginning. Through him all things were made; without him nothing was made that has been made. In him was life, and that life was the light of all mankind. The light shines in the darkness, and the darkness has not overcome it.

JOHN 1:1–5 NIV

God's Word is powerful because *God is His Word*. That sounds mysterious, doesn't it? That's where faith comes in. Hebrews 4:12 tells us God's Word is living and active and sharper than a two-edged sword. The more we study His Word and the more we incorporate it into our lives, the more of His power we have.

When Jesus was tempted by Satan, He spoke God's Word. Satan was no match for God's power. We have access to that same power, but we can't take advantage of it if we don't know it. Read His Word. Display it on the walls of your home. Listen to music that incorporates His promises into the lyrics. Fill your heart, mind, and spirit with God's Word, and watch His transforming power take over your life.

Thank You for Your living Word, Father. I want Your power in my life. When I think I'm too busy to spend time in Your Word, remind me of its power. I want more of You.

SEEKERS AND FINDERS

Turning around, Jesus saw them following and asked, "What do you want?" They said, "Rabbi" (which means "Teacher"), "where are you staying?" "Come," he replied, "and you will see." So they went and saw where he was staying, and they spent that day with him. It was about four in the afternoon.
JOHN 1:38–39 NIV

John the Baptist—Jesus' cousin—had many followers before Jesus began His ministry. In these verses, Jesus had just walked past John with a couple of His students, and John said, "Behold, the Lamb of God, who takes away the sin of the world!" (John 1:29). The students were curious, so they followed Jesus.

One of these guys was Peter, who became one of Jesus' most loyal followers. Peter was responsible for much of the growth of the early church after Jesus' death and resurrection. And it all started because he made the decision to follow Jesus.

Jeremiah 29:13 tells us that if we seek God with all our hearts, we will find Him. Peter was a seeker here, and as a result, he was a finder. That same promise is true for us today. If we're looking for God, we will find Him if we look with sincerity and persistence.

What are you looking for? If you search for wealth, you may or may not find it. If you pursue fame, it may or may not happen. But if you seek God, He promises you'll be successful. He's not hiding from you. More than anything, He wants to be found.

With all my heart, I want to find You, Lord.

WHAT DOES HE SEE?

When Jesus saw Nathanael approaching, he said of him, "Here truly is an Israelite in whom there is no deceit." "How do you know me?" Nathanael asked. Jesus answered, "I saw you while you were still under the fig tree before Philip called you."
JOHN 1:47–48 NIV

At this point, early in His ministry, Jesus was looking for a few good men. When He saw Nathanael, He said, "Now here's a guy I can trust." What a lovely thing to say!

Nathanael didn't have to try to impress Jesus. The Lord already knew everything about him. He knows all there is to know about each of us too. When He looks in your heart, what does He see? Maybe you're loyal and a good friend. Maybe you're a hard worker. Maybe you're great with numbers or an excellent chef. Whatever you are, He sees. He knows. And He wants you on His team. He will take your gifts and talents and abilities, all your character traits and even your flaws, and use them for good and for His glory. And whatever your weaknesses, He'll fill them in with His strength.

Will you answer His call?

Sometimes I wonder what You see in me, Lord. I hope, as with Nathanael, You see an honest person who wants to serve You. But whatever You see, whatever I am, I give to You. I'm Yours. I want to serve You with all I am.

THIRSTY

On the last and greatest day of the festival, Jesus stood and said in a loud voice, "Let anyone who is thirsty come to me and drink. Whoever believes in me, as Scripture has said, rivers of living water will flow from within them."
JOHN 7:37–38 NIV

The Festival of Booths, also known as the Feast of Tabernacles, was a weeklong festival that happened each year. Every native-born male of Israel was required to attend. Jesus' brothers tried to get Him to go with them, but Jesus knew that people were trying to kill Him and that it wasn't His time to die yet. So He told them to go on without Him. He went later, but He stayed hidden.

On the last day, Jesus wanted everyone to know who He was. They didn't have to keep offering sacrifices—He was the sacrifice. If they came to Him, their thirst for God would be quenched. Through Christ, our relationship with God is restored once and for all. We don't have to jump through hoops or follow difficult rituals anymore. He took care of everything.

Are you thirsty for God? Quench that thirst with Jesus. Immerse yourself in His Word. Soak in His love, and let His rivers of living water flow through your veins.

I'm thirsty for You, Lord, and I need to be quenched.
Thank You for Your sacrifice for me. Let Your
presence flow like water through my soul.

SET FREE

Jesus replied, "Very truly I tell you, everyone who sins is a slave to sin. Now a slave has no permanent place in the family, but a son belongs to it forever. So if the Son sets you free, you will be free indeed."
JOHN 8:34–36 NIV

Most of us reading this book would denounce slavery as inhumane. Yet many of us choose to remain slaves, even after being set free. This verse tells us that we all sin. And sin rules our desires, our thoughts, and our actions. Because we're human, we're born into slavery. We don't have a chance, unless we're set free.

Jesus came to set us free. He breaks sin's power over us so that we have a choice. We don't have to be ruled by addiction, fear, anxiety, depression, anger, greed, or any other sinful thing. But because our current state feels safe and familiar, many of us choose to remain in slavery to our sin. Being set free means change, and change can feel uncomfortable at first. It takes work. It takes learning a different way of life. But it is, oh, so worth the effort.

You've been set free. Are you living in freedom?

Help me live, breathe, and walk in Your freedom, Lord. Teach me the skills I need to navigate this new way of life in You.

ABUNDANT LIFE

The thief comes only to steal and kill and destroy; I have come that they may have life, and have it to the full.
JOHN 10:10 NIV

Jesus didn't just come so we could live with Him for eternity after we die. That's an amazing perk, but His blessings are for right here, right now. He wants us to live a full life. Some translations say He came so that we could have *abundant* life. According to Dictionary.com, *abundant* means "richly supplied" or "oversufficient."

Yet there's a thief lurking around every corner, trying to steal your abundance. He wants to kill your joy and snuff out your peace. Don't let him! Thieves like to do their work in darkness, so shine your light. Fill up on God's Word. Speak it, think it, pray it. That will send the thief—Satan—running every time.

But he will be back. He *always* comes back. So stay close to Jesus. Let His presence beam. And take hold of the abundant life—full of love, joy, peace, and more blessings than you can count—that God intended for His children to live on this earth.

I'm afraid I've left the door open for the thief, Lord. He's come in and stolen my joy. I live in depression and anxiety, and I'm tired of it. Teach me to be on guard against Satan and help me take hold of the abundant life You want me to live.

WAITING

Now Jesus loved Martha and her sister and Lazarus. So when he heard that Lazarus was sick, he stayed where he was two more days.

JOHN 11:5–6 NIV

We're not sure how Jesus came to be so close to Mary, Martha, and Lazarus. However it came about, the relationship between Jesus and this family was special. So when Jesus got the news that Lazarus was gravely ill, it would make sense for Him to jump up and go to His friend right away. But He didn't.

By the time Jesus arrived, Lazarus had already died. Martha met Jesus outside and asked what many of us would have asked: "Where have You been? If You'd come sooner, Lazarus wouldn't be dead" (see John 11:21).

But if Jesus had come right away and healed Lazarus, we wouldn't have the story of this amazing miracle. Jesus raised His friend from the dead, showing His power over death.

Sometimes we wonder why Jesus doesn't act right away when we call on Him. But if He gives us what we want the moment we ask, we may miss the miracle, the victory, and the glory that come from waiting on God's perfect timing. Living a life free of hardships and trials can get pretty boring. . .and God wants us to live an abundant life, filled with stories of His power, glory, and grace.

Teach me to wait, Lord. I trust You, and I know You are good.

PARTICIPATION COUNTS!

Jesus, once more deeply moved, came to the tomb. It was a cave with a stone laid across the entrance. "Take away the stone," he said. "But, Lord," said Martha, the sister of the dead man, "by this time there is a bad odor, for he has been there four days." Then Jesus said, "Did I not tell you that if you believe, you will see the glory of God?" So they took away the stone. Then Jesus looked up and said, "Father, I thank you that you have heard me."

JOHN 11:38–41 NIV

During Bible times, it was customary to bury loved ones in a cave and to seal the cave with a heavy stone to protect the body. Jesus was God in the flesh, so He could have moved the stone by Himself. He didn't need anyone's help. Yet He told whoever was listening—probably His disciples—to take away the stone.

Jesus doesn't *need* our help to fulfill His purpose and plans. But He wants us to be involved! He gives each of us a part to play so we can be involved in His story. He doesn't want us to view life from the sidelines. Remember, He has an abundant life planned for us, filled with stories of God's glory. He wants us to be participants, not spectators.

What is your role in His story?

I want to roll away the stone, Lord—or do whatever You need me to do. I want to play an active role in Your story.

ABIDE

"If you abide in me, and my words abide in you, ask whatever you wish, and it will be done for you. By this my Father is glorified, that you bear much fruit and so prove to be my disciples. As the Father has loved me, so have I loved you. Abide in my love."

JOHN 15:7–9

To understand these verses, we first must understand what it means to *abide*. This word means to remain, continue, or stay. It can also mean to have one's abode, to dwell, or to reside. Other definitions include to endure, to sustain, or to wait for something.

With those definitions in mind, reread today's passage. If we remain in, live in, and wait for Christ, and if His words remain in and live in us, we can ask anything, and He will do it. It's a free pass, but there's a catch. When we truly abide in Christ and fill our hearts, minds, and spirits with His living Word, our desires change. He infuses us to the point that we want what He wants. And the things we ask Him for will be the things we need to live out His plan for our lives.

He gives us what we ask for so we can glorify the Father and bear much fruit—meaning we take on His character and lead others to His love.

What will you ask Him for today? Abide in Him and see if your desires change. He will give you whatever you need to fulfill His purpose for you.

Teach me to abide in You, Lord.

STAND DOWN

Then Simon Peter, who had a sword, drew it and struck the high priest's servant, cutting off his right ear. (The servant's name was Malchus.) Jesus commanded Peter, "Put your sword away! Shall I not drink the cup the Father has given me?"
JOHN 18:10–11 NIV

At first reading, Simon Peter's actions may seem heroic. He's defending his Lord. He wasn't about to let them take Jesus without a fight. But Jesus scolded Peter: "Put your sword away!" Why didn't He commend Peter? Why didn't He thank him for his loyalty?

When faced with difficult circumstances, many of us are like Peter. We need to *do* something. And when we don't know what to do, we fight. But God wants us to be still. The battle belongs to the Lord (Deuteronomy 20:4). There are times He *orders* us to fight, so *fighting* isn't the issue. The problem occurs when we go ahead of the Lord and try to take things into our own hands.

What are you facing today? Are you tempted to move forward without waiting on God? Stand down. Put away your sword. Wait for God's direction. Until then, let Him fight your battles.

I'm guilty of moving ahead of You, Lord, and I'm sorry. Teach me to be still and wait. I know You're my defender. When You're ready for me to act, make it clear. Until then, I'll stand right here.

RESPOND, DON'T REACT

Then Pilate went back into his headquarters and called for Jesus to be brought to him. "Are you the king of the Jews?" he asked him. Jesus replied, "Is this your own question, or did others tell you about me?" "Am I a Jew?" Pilate retorted. "Your own people and their leading priests brought you to me for trial. Why? What have you done?" Jesus answered, "My Kingdom is not an earthly kingdom. If it were, my followers would fight to keep me from being handed over to the Jewish leaders. But my Kingdom is not of this world."

JOHN 18:33–36 NLT

Anyone who's ever felt attacked or bullied or had their integrity wrongly questioned can relate to what Jesus must have felt in this moment. But Jesus' response goes against human nature. While most in this situation would react defensively and in anger, Jesus stayed calm. He answered with wisdom.

While some may look at this account and think Jesus' response didn't help because He still was crucified, truly it made all the difference. His credibility was enhanced because of His choice to remain serene and not get angry. If He'd lost control, it would have given everyone, for the rest of time, reason to question His authenticity.

When you feel attacked, remain calm. Either speak with wisdom or say nothing. Respond, don't react. In the moment, it may feel like you're losing the battle. But in the long run, like Jesus, you'll end up the winner.

**When people anger me, Father,
help me respond with love and wisdom.**

CHRISTIANS EVERYWHERE

Afterward Joseph of Arimathea, who had been a secret disciple of Jesus (because he feared the Jewish leaders), asked Pilate for permission to take down Jesus' body. When Pilate gave permission, Joseph came and took the body away. With him came Nicodemus, the man who had come to Jesus at night. He brought about seventy-five pounds of perfumed ointment made from myrrh and aloes.
JOHN 19:38–39 NLT

Joseph of Arimathea believed Jesus was God's Son. But until this point, he'd kept quiet about his faith because he was afraid of the repercussions. In the same way, Nicodemus, a Pharisee and a member of the Sanhedrin (Israel's judicial council), was a secret follower of Christ. These men remained in the shadows until God showed them it was time to take their faith public. At just the right time, they stepped forward and said, "I believe, and I refuse to hide it anymore."

There are Christ followers everywhere. That's why Christianity has spread throughout the world and survived thousands of years. If you feel alone in your faith, ask God to send you a believing friend. Ask Him to help you find each other. You never know—they might be praying for the same thing.

I need Christian friends, Lord. I need people I can feel safe with, who will accept me and support me and help me grow in faith. Teach me to be that kind of friend for others. Reveal other Christians who may be closer than I imagined so we can support each other.

GENEROUS

*All the believers were united in heart and mind.
And they felt that what they owned was not their
own, so they shared everything they had.*

ACTS 4:32 NLT

In today's politically charged climate, a lot of people are talking about socialism. Some people are in favor of it, believing everyone should be given the same things. Others are against it, because they feel socialism forces hard workers to support those who don't work. The people in the early church lived a form of voluntary socialism as opposed to political socialism.

What's the difference? you may ask. An important distinction is the word *voluntary*. Members of the early church experienced their own type of cancel culture. Once it was known that someone was a Christian, many would stop doing business with them. Without the help and support of other Christians, they may have starved. They certainly would have gone without having many of their basic needs met.

So they propped each other up. They didn't hoard their belongings but shared with those in need. They saw themselves as a family, and they looked out for each other. No one forced them. They did it because they wanted to.

God approves of such generosity. If the government or a church council or any other body forces us to give, where's the blessing in that? God generously and willingly sacrificed His only Son for us, and He loves to see us willingly pour out our abundance for others in need.

Teach me to be wise and generous with Your blessings, Lord.

AUTHENTIC

But there was a certain man named Ananias who, with his wife, Sapphira, sold some property. He brought part of the money to the apostles, claiming it was the full amount. With his wife's consent, he kept the rest.
ACTS 5:1–2 NLT

This is the beginning of Ananias and Sapphira's story. The ending is severe. The middle tells us that they deliberately lied about the value of the property and how much they gave to the church. Even when questioned about it, they clung to their lie.

This couple wasn't punished because they kept some of the earnings for themselves. It was their money. They could do with it whatever they wanted. They were punished for *lying*. They tried to convince people they'd given everything. They were punished for being inauthentic, for trying to come across as holy and godly and more generous than they were. It was the *fakeness* of it all that angered God.

Proverbs 6:16–17 tells us God hates a lying tongue, while 2 Corinthians 9:7 says God loves a cheerful giver. We all have different gifts, different amounts of time, and different finances, and God will show each of us what He wants us to give to Him and others. We're not required to give it *all*, except in special circumstances. But whatever we give, we should give with joy and humility. . .not to try to make ourselves look good.

I'm sorry for trying to impress others, Lord. Teach me to be authentic.

REGRET

Saul was one of the witnesses, and he agreed completely with the killing of Stephen. A great wave of persecution began that day, sweeping over the church in Jerusalem; and all the believers except the apostles were scattered through the regions of Judea and Samaria. (Some devout men came and buried Stephen with great mourning.) But Saul was going everywhere to destroy the church. He went from house to house, dragging out both men and women to throw them into prison.

ACTS 8:1–3 NLT

Some of us may think we have a checkered past. But few, if any, of us live with the regret Paul must have felt. Also known as Saul, he was an extremely religious person who lacked a true relationship with God. He hated Christians because they didn't follow the set rules of Judaism. He was an extremist.

Then he met Christ, and everything changed. God sent him to spread the gospel to the Gentiles—people who weren't Jewish.

Regret is hard, but it's not always a bad thing. Letting our past mistakes paralyze us is what is truly unfortunate. Instead, like Paul, we can let our regret fuel our determination to change. Paul used his guilt to energize his desire to make things right and to carry on God's work.

What regrets do you have? How might they inform your ability to serve God and bring others to Him?

Thank You for turning my past mistakes into opportunities to serve You, Lord. I'm Yours—mistakes and all—to use however You see fit.

THE BLESSING CYCLE

So the believers in Antioch decided to send relief to the brothers and sisters in Judea, everyone giving as much as they could. This they did, entrusting their gifts to Barnabas and Saul to take to the elders of the church in Jerusalem.
ACTS 11:29–30 NLT

When you get a little extra cash, how do you use it? Do you save it, spend it, or share it with others? It's natural—and not wrong—to buy something special for yourself now and then. But God designed a mysterious little life hack that is counterintuitive to our human nature. Giving to others—especially to those in need—brings us more joy and deeper satisfaction than spending money on our own pleasure.

God wants us to experience this kind of fulfillment so much that He often blesses us for this purpose. He gives us extra because He wants us to share with other people. It's fun to play a game with the concept. Give generously, then wait and watch to see how God gives your gift back to you so you can give it away again!

He doesn't always bless with cash. You may have an old car in your garage that never gets driven. See who you can bless, and watch the blessings come back to you. Maybe it's a nice-but-seldom-worn outfit or that set of dishes boxed up in the hall closet. Bless others and watch how He blesses you. Keep the cycle going, and your heart will fill with more joy than you thought possible.

Father, thank You for blessing me so I can bless others.

THE IMPORTANCE OF BEING EARNEST

Then he imprisoned him, placing him under the guard of four squads of four soldiers each. Herod intended to bring Peter out for public trial after the Passover. But while Peter was in prison, the church prayed very earnestly for him.
ACTS 12:4–5 NLT

What is the difference between *prayer* and *earnest prayer*? According to Dictionary.com, one definition of *earnest* is "showing depth and sincerity of feeling." Hopefully all our prayers are sincere. But 1 Thessalonians 5:17 tells us to "pray without ceasing." God wants us to chat with Him as we go about our daily business, but not all prayer can be on-your-knees, tears-in-your-eyes earnest. After all, we have obligations to meet, bills to pay, kitchens to clean.

God is interested in all our prayers. But when things get serious, when we pray *earnestly* as the church prayed for Peter, God gets serious as well. He figures if it's important enough to us to fall on our faces and cry out to Him, it's important to Him too. He longs to be the first one we turn to for help, and when we pray earnestly, we're admitting that we're helpless and He is our only hope.

What do you need from God today? Stop what you're doing and really *talk* to Him. Tell Him you're desperate for Him. Beg Him to help you. He loves you, and His love will never let you down.

**Father, You are my only hope.
I need You to act, and I trust Your love.**

ENCOURAGER

The messengers went at once to Antioch, where they called a general meeting of the believers and delivered the letter. And there was great joy throughout the church that day as they read this encouraging message. Then Judas and Silas, both being prophets, spoke at length to the believers, encouraging and strengthening their faith.
Acts 15:30–32 NLT

When was the last time you received a letter in the mail that made you smile? Maybe it was an email or a text message. When we receive an encouraging word from a friend, things just feel a little lighter. We're reminded that we're not alone in this world and that others are praying for us, cheering for us, and hoping for our best.

Since we know what a difference an encouraging word can make, it's important to ask ourselves: *Am I an encourager? When was the last time I went out of my way to make someone smile, give them hope, and remind them they're not alone?*

In the beginning, God decided it wasn't good for us to be alone. He made Adam a suitable partner, and since then we've lived in communities. We need each other. We rely on each other. God designed us to lean on and support one another. If you haven't consciously made the effort to encourage others in writing or speech, do it today. It will lift someone else's spirits and yours too!

Remind me to be an encourager, Lord.

DISAGREEMENTS

But Paul did not think it wise to take him, because he had deserted them in Pamphylia and had not continued with them in the work. They had such a sharp disagreement that they parted company. Barnabas took Mark and sailed for Cyprus, but Paul chose Silas and left, commended by the believers to the grace of the Lord. He went through Syria and Cilicia, strengthening the churches.
ACTS 15:38–41 NIV

It really stinks when we have disagreements with people we care about. Sometimes these things happen because of pride and selfishness. But what about when there's an honest difference of opinion? Sometimes neither person is wrong. . .they just disagree.

On an earlier trip, Mark made a decision that Paul didn't agree with. Later, when Barnabas wanted to take Mark along on a journey, Paul refused. So Barnabas and Mark went one way and Paul and Silas went another. Their honest disagreement caused a speedier and more thorough spread of the gospel.

When we're at odds with someone, it can be difficult to see how God could use that. But trust Him. He can turn any situation around and use it for good.

When I disagree with someone, my pride often gets in the way. I think I'm right and they're wrong. Remind me that sometimes people just see things differently. Help me to always act in a way that honors You. I trust You to bring good from all things, even disagreements.

POWERFUL WOMEN

And some of them were persuaded and joined Paul and Silas, as did a great many of the devout Greeks and not a few of the leading women. . . . Many of them therefore believed, with not a few Greek women of high standing as well as men.

ACTS 17:4, 12

In today's passage, "not a few" means "many." These leading, influential Greek women were among the first Gentile believers, and their influence and standing in the community heavily assisted the spread of the gospel. It's interesting that at a time in history when most of us picture women as being without rights, Luke (the author of Acts) included this bit of information. It provides yet another indication that God's daughters are powerful!

We don't know who these leading women were. They may have been businesswomen and socialites and wives of government officials. They may have been women of high character who'd earned trust through a lifetime of trying to do the right thing. We can be sure that these women multiplied Paul and Silas' efforts to share the good news of Jesus Christ—that's why they're mentioned in the book of Acts.

What is your circle of influence? No matter how great or small your influence, your life affects others. Use your words, your actions, your life to share the love of Christ. As God's child, you are powerful.

Sometimes I forget about the amount of influence I have on the people around me. Help me use that sway to point people to You.

NOT MY OWN

But I do not consider my life of any account as dear to myself, so that I may finish my course and the ministry which I received from the Lord Jesus, to testify solemnly of the gospel of God's grace.
ACTS 20:24 NASB

This passage comes from an account of one of Paul's messages as he spoke to the elders at the church in Ephesus. He basically said, "My life isn't really mine to live as I please. It belongs to God, and I'm here to do as He tells me." Before becoming a Christ follower, Paul (then Saul) did some awful things. After committing his life to Christ, he experienced prison, hunger, illness, shipwrecks, and many other severe hardships. And that was okay with him, because he was on a mission to share the good news he'd found for himself.

Life can be hard. It has its joyful times, but it's also full of trials. Either we can hold on to our perceived right to have everything go our way, and be miserable when it doesn't, or we can take Paul's approach. We can recognize that we've been placed here, in this specific time and place and with our exact temperament, gifts, and abilities, to do God's work. We are here to live out His purpose, which is to love others and point them to a relationship with Him. Our fullest reward will come when we get to heaven. Until then, our lives are not our own.

**Thank You for making me Your child, Father.
My life is Yours to do with as You please.**

SHIPWRECKED

*When it was decided that we would sail for Italy,
they proceeded to turn Paul and some other prisoners
over to a centurion of the Augustan cohort, named Julius.*
ACTS 27:1 NASB

Paul was a prisoner. It was decided *for* him that he'd go to Italy. He didn't get to make that choice for himself. On the journey, there was a severe storm that led to a shipwreck. It wasn't a pleasant trip, to say the least.

Though a relationship with Christ brings freedom from sin, we don't always get to make decisions about what happens to us. Sometimes things are decided for us, and many times those things are not pleasant. But whatever comes, it helps to remember that our King is in control. He determines which way our lives go. Either we can rebel against Him, or we can willingly submit to His plan for our lives. Things will be a lot easier and more peaceful if we trust Him and obey without fighting. When we choose to follow Him willingly, we can be assured that He'll work out all things for our good and His glory.

Right now my life feels like a shipwreck, Lord. I'm not enjoying this part of the journey. But I still trust You. While I can see only right now, You see the big picture. I know You have good things in store for my life.

WHEN HOPE IS GONE

The soldiers' plan was to kill the prisoners, so that none of them would swim away and escape; but the centurion, wanting to bring Paul safely through, kept them from accomplishing their intention, and commanded that those who could swim were to jump overboard first and get to land.
ACTS 27:42–43 NASB

When Paul's boat was shipwrecked, the guards were worried the prisoners would escape. If that happened, the guards would be severely punished. They decided it would be easier just to kill the prisoners than risk the consequences. But the centurion (or captain) was fond of Paul. He kept the guards from harming any of the prisoners. Instead, he encouraged everyone to swim for their lives.

Sometimes it may seem like there's no hope, like we have no way out of our current situation. But God is always in control! He will send people to show us kindness and support just when we need it. He'll open doors, change circumstances, and part seas (Exodus 14). With God, there is always hope.

There's another thing to consider in this story. What kind of hope do we offer others? Look around. Do you see someone who's struggling, who feels like there's no way out? How can you help them? How can you be the centurion, offering solutions and hope to those who can't help themselves?

Father, thank You for this reminder—with You, there is hope. Help me offer hope to those around me who are struggling.

FROM FAITH TO FAITH

For I am not ashamed of the gospel, for it is the power of God for salvation to everyone who believes, to the Jew first and also to the Greek. For in it the righteousness of God is revealed from faith to faith; as it is written: "But the righteous one will live by faith."
ROMANS 1:16–17 NASB

In today's culture, we may not be *ashamed* of the gospel. . .but we might feel afraid to let others know of our beliefs. After all, Christians are often judged harshly, and people may not like us for that one reason alone.

But we should never be ashamed or afraid to talk about our relationship with Christ. Our faith brings God's power to life in us! The phrase "from faith to faith" refers to the way faith grows. A little bit of faith leads to more faith, which leads to even greater faith. The act of having faith produces more faith.

The author also reminds us of an Old Testament verse, Habakkuk 2:4 (NASB): "But the righteous one will live by his faith." Faith makes us righteous, which gives us more faith, which makes us more righteous. . . . It's a beautiful cycle that propels us into right standing with God, which includes the full blessings of His power, His hope, and His peace.

Thank You for giving me a seed of faith as a starting point, Father. Help me share that faith with others. I want my faith to grow strong.

BE A DOER

For it is not the hearers of the law who are righteous before God, but the doers of the law who will be justified.
ROMANS 2:13

Many of the people reading Paul's letter to the Roman Christians had grown up in the Jewish faith. They'd had scripture read to them since they were small children, and they mistakenly thought that because they were familiar with God's Word, they were righteous. Paul wanted to clear up this misconception. Simply hearing the Word of God doesn't make anyone godly. It's *obedience* to God's Word that puts us in right standing with God.

The same is true today. Many churches have people sitting in the pews, listening to sermons week after week. But once they exit the church doors, they keep living their lives however they please. They think that because they go to a worship service, they're "in." But that's not how it works.

Hearing God's Word is the seed. But acting on His Word causes it to take root and grow. Just as a dry seed on the ground doesn't do any good on its own, the Bible, falling on deaf ears, won't produce righteousness. If we want to please God, we must obey Him.

Thank You for Your Word, Father. I want it to take root in my life and grow. I know that the more I obey Your Word by loving You and others, the more I'll please You. Teach me to obey.

CIRCUMCISED

For he is not a Jew who is one outwardly, nor is circumcision that which is outward in the flesh. But he is a Jew who is one inwardly; and circumcision is of the heart, by the Spirit, not by the letter; and his praise is not from people, but from God.
ROMANS 2:28–29 NASB

God commanded males in the Jewish faith to be circumcised. Circumcision is cutting away the extra flesh to keep the inner flesh clean. It's a painful process, as you can imagine. In this passage, Paul explains to his readers—both Jews and Gentiles—that the outer, physical act of circumcision is only a symbol of what God really wants from us.

Circumcision of the heart, as Paul refers to it here, is the (often painful) process of cutting away the extra, unnecessary fleshly desires and concerns to keep our hearts clean. It involves denying our sinful nature, saying no to things that don't please God, and choosing to live pure, clean lives. It's not easy to deny our human wants. But just as an unclean body can cause infection and illness, an unclean heart leads to spiritual disease and death.

Ask God to help you get rid of anything that prevents you from having a right relationship with Him.

Father, I want to be clean, pure, and healthy before You. It's hard to turn my back on my anxieties and addictions, but I'll do whatever it takes to please You.

BELIEVE

For what does the Scripture say? "Abraham believed God, and it was credited to him as righteousness."... In hope against hope he believed, so that he might become a father of many nations according to that which had been spoken, "So shall your descendants be." Without becoming weak in faith he contemplated his own body, now as good as dead since he was about a hundred years old, and the deadness of Sarah's womb; yet, with respect to the promise of God, he did not waver in unbelief but grew strong in faith, giving glory to God, and being fully assured that what God had promised, He was able also to perform. Therefore it was also credited to him as righteousness.

ROMANS 4:3, 18–22 NASB

Has God placed a dream in your heart—something that seems impossible, yet you know it's from Him? That's what happened to Abraham. He was nearly one hundred years old, and his wife, Sarah, was too old to have children as well. Yet God promised to make Abraham's descendants as numerous as the stars. Abraham could have rolled his eyes and said, "Yeah, right." Instead, he believed. He figured if God said it, it would happen. This kind of faith pleases God.

What has God promised you? Believe Him and wait for it to happen.

Your promises give me hope, Lord. But the voices in my head often tell me not to believe, not to hope, not to expect too much. Silence those negative voices. I choose to believe You.

THE THING ABOUT FAITH

And without faith it is impossible to please Him, for the one who comes to God must believe that He exists, and that He proves to be One who rewards those who seek Him.
HEBREWS 11:6 NASB

It would be easy to take this verse out of context, advocating for blind faith. But true faith is a hefty, gritty, sweaty process. It involves believing in our hearts and minds and letting that faith fuel our actions.

Blind faith might say, "I know God will take care of my needs, so I'll just stay home and sleep all day and trust God to pay my bills and put food on the table." But true faith says, "God knows I need a job, so I trust Him to provide work that suits my abilities and needs." Then faith acts on that belief by applying for jobs, working hard, and showing gratitude for the chance to contribute to your family and society.

Without faith, it's impossible to please God. If faith were easy—if it were a free ticket to all our desires—everyone would choose faith. Instead, faith is believing when it doesn't make human sense to believe. . .and acting as though what we believe is already reality. How are you living out your faith today?

I believe Your promises, Lord. Show me practical ways to act on that faith. I know You will always keep Your Word. I also know You want me to live as though I truly believe what You say. Thank You for keeping Your promises to me.

SET YOUR MIND

For those who are in accord with the flesh set their minds on the things of the flesh, but those who are in accord with the Spirit, the things of the Spirit. For the mind set on the flesh is death, but the mind set on the Spirit is life and peace, because the mind set on the flesh is hostile toward God; for it does not subject itself to the law of God, for it is not even able to do so, and those who are in the flesh cannot please God.

ROMANS 8:5–8 NASB

If we could learn to control our thoughts, it would change everything. Those voices in our heads drive our moods, our attitudes, and our actions. Though we can't prevent random thoughts from flitting through our minds, it's important to recognize that thoughts are just thoughts. They're like gnats or mosquitoes. We can swat them away.

If we leave stagnant water in a bucket on the porch, we'll invite those nasty bugs. But if we keep a clean and dry physical environment, we make it hard for the bugs to stay. Our thoughts are the same! When we set our minds on sinful things, such as anger, anxieties, or addictions, we invite negative thoughts. But when we focus on God and His Word, when we seek Him above all else, we create a healthy environment in our minds, fertile for His peace, love, and abundant life.

Help me focus my thoughts on You, Lord. I want Your life, Your peace, and Your love to fill my heart and mind.

MORE THAN CONQUERORS

What then shall we say to these things? If God is for us, who can be against us? ... Who shall separate us from the love of Christ? Shall tribulation, or distress, or persecution, or famine, or nakedness, or danger, or sword? ... No, in all these things we are more than conquerors through him who loved us.

ROMANS 8:31, 35, 37

Some people view Christianity as one long beach vacation, relaxing in the sand, listening to soft waves lap against the shore. They see it as a sweet, calm, peaceful existence, free of adversity. While God certainly provides rest when we need it, He wants more for us. His children are fighters. Heroes. Conquerors.

You can't be a conqueror unless there's something to conquer. As Christ-followers, we will face hard things. We are enemies of Satan, and he's at war with us. He will try everything in his power to make us renounce our faith. But with faith, we will not be defeated! We aren't just conquerors; we are *more than conquerors*. We don't just win against Satan. With God, we *beat him*. We knock him flat and pin him to the ground with one foot. We are strong and mighty warriors in the most powerful army in existence.

What difficulties do you face? What tools does Satan use to bring you down? Stand strong. Trust God. Fight with His promises. God is more powerful than the enemy, and His power lives in you.

Thank You for making me a warrior, a fighter, and a victor, Lord. When I get discouraged, please remind me who I am.

ABSOLUTELY NOTHING

For I am sure that neither death nor life, nor angels nor rulers, nor things present nor things to come, nor powers, nor height nor depth, nor anything else in all creation, will be able to separate us from the love of God in Christ Jesus our Lord.

ROMANS 8:38–39

Many people, even those with strong faith, worry that they may somehow lose God's love for them. Paul writes to assure his readers—both then and now—that God's commitment to us is solid, permanent, and unwavering. Nothing in this life or beyond can shake His love from us.

Paul begins his list in today's passage with death. On this side of heaven, death brings permanent separation. When a loved one dies, we know we'll never see them in human form again. Yet for the believer in Christ, death only brings us more fully into God's presence than we've ever known before.

There's not a single life circumstance that will cause God to stop loving us. There's no king powerful enough, no angel or demon strong enough, no ocean deep enough to sever us from our connection with Him. No spaceship can soar so high that we're off His radar. Absolutely *nothing* can separate us from God's eternal, overwhelming love for us.

Thank You for loving me in a way I can't fathom, Lord. I love You too, with all my heart.

THE PROCESS OF FAITH

*So faith comes from hearing,
and hearing through the word of Christ.*
ROMANS 10:17

Picture a wooden bucket positioned under an old water pump. It's filled with nasty, stagnant water. Algae clings to the sides and floats on top, and mosquitoes lay their larvae on the surface. But if we pump clean water into that bucket, the old, dirty water will eventually spill over the sides. As we continue, all the gross water will be forced out and replaced with fresh, pure water. That's what God's Word does to our lives.

Earlier in this letter, Paul told his readers not only to be hearers of God's Word but to be doers. Here he tells us that faith comes from hearing. So which is it?

Faith involves both hearing and doing. We first must hear God's Word if we want to put it into practice. When we read and listen to God's Word as often as possible, when we pour His promises into our lives, it changes us. As His promises flow into our spirits, the old, stagnant way of thinking is forced out. Soon we're filled with a pure, clear, nourishing faith.

Thank You for making Your Word so accessible to me, Father. I'm sorry for neglecting my time with You. Pour Your Word into me, forcing out my stagnant way of thinking. Grow in me a strong faith that fuels my actions.

KIND AND SEVERE

Note then the kindness and the severity of God: severity toward those who have fallen, but God's kindness to you, provided you continue in his kindness. Otherwise you too will be cut off. And even they, if they do not continue in their unbelief, will be grafted in, for God has the power to graft them in again.

ROMANS 11:22–23

At first glance, Paul's words here can seem terrifying. If God is severe toward those who've fallen, doesn't that include all of us? We all mess up sometimes.

But Paul's emphasis isn't on God's severity or His kindness. It's on our *faith*. Our relationship with God rests entirely on our belief in His Son, Jesus Christ. With faith, God is kind. He invites all who believe to join His family as His full children. But if we reject His Son, He will cut us off and cast us aside. There is no way to have a good relationship with God except through His Son.

But His kindness gives us hope. Even if we fall away for a time, we can always come back. He longs for a relationship with us, and through faith in Jesus Christ, He will always graft us back into the family tree.

Thank You for Your kindness, Father. I'm so grateful to be Your child. May I never turn my back on You or fall away from You. But I know if I do, and then I sincerely regret it, You'll always welcome me home.

BEYOND COMPREHENSION

Oh, the depth of the riches and wisdom and knowledge of God! How unsearchable are his judgments and how inscrutable his ways!
ROMANS 11:33

Most of us who own and drive cars don't understand all the intricacies of how they work. We simply get in the car, start it, and drive it to our destination. We don't have to understand all the ins and outs of mechanics to appreciate and take advantage of our cars' amazing properties.

The same is true for computers, airplane travel, and so many other things. We may not understand them, but we're glad they exist. We're grateful for the benefits they give us.

We will never fully understand God's magnitude. We can't comprehend His wisdom and purpose for all things. . .but we know He's real. We know His love is unending. We can rely on His plan and trust He has everything under control. He has a destination in mind, and He will get us there. In the meantime, our job is to believe Him, thank Him for His goodness, and rest in His love.

Father, I'm so grateful for Your wisdom, and I trust all Your decisions for my life. I'm thankful for the riches of Your grace, and I know You'll provide everything I need. I don't always understand the things that happen, but I know You are good and all Your actions are based in love. I worship You.

LIVING SACRIFICE

I appeal to you therefore, brothers, by the mercies of God, to present your bodies as a living sacrifice, holy and acceptable to God, which is your spiritual worship. Do not be conformed to this world, but be transformed by the renewal of your mind, that by testing you may discern what is the will of God, what is good and acceptable and perfect.

ROMANS 12:1–2

Before Christ came, the Jewish people had to offer animal sacrifices to God. They'd kill the animals and give them to God as a form of worship. But then Christ came. He died on the cross once for all, providing a full and final sacrifice. We don't have to offer *killed* sacrifices anymore, because Jesus offered Himself for us.

We're called to give our bodies as *living* sacrifices. He wants us to submit our thoughts, words, and actions to Him. Christ is now seated on the throne in heaven, and the only physical body He has on earth is ours. When we ask Him to let His thoughts be our thoughts and to let His ways be our ways, we magnify His presence in the world. The more we allow Him to fill us by reading His Word and doing His work, the more our minds are transformed. We take on a family resemblance as we start to look like our Father.

Jesus, thank You for sacrificing Yourself so I can fully live. In return, I offer my body, mind, and spirit to You for You to use however You want. Make me an instrument of Your love here on earth.

ONE BODY

For by the grace given to me I say to everyone among you not to think of himself more highly than he ought to think, but to think with sober judgment, each according to the measure of faith that God has assigned. For as in one body we have many members, and the members do not all have the same function, so we, though many, are one body in Christ, and individually members one of another.

Romans 12:3–5

Pride is one of the greatest downfalls of most humans. Even those of us with good manners, who have the decency not to flaunt our pride, often secretly think *we're* right and others are wrong. We think we're better than others.

But Paul warns against comparing ourselves with others. Comparison only breeds envy, which makes us miserable. Instead, Paul wants us to remember that we each have an important role in God's kingdom.

If you bought a large home, and every room in that home was a bathroom, you wouldn't be able to cook meals for your family. You wouldn't have a comfortable place to sleep or play board games. In a similar way, God has given each of His children different skills and circumstances so His plan can be fully accomplished. We all play significant roles in fulfilling God's purpose. Be careful about thinking you're better than anyone else or thinking anyone else is better than you.

Forgive me for my pride, Lord. Teach me to use my gifts fully and to appreciate what others have to offer.

FINDING YOUR GIFTS

Having gifts that differ according to the grace given to us, let us use them: if prophecy, in proportion to our faith; if service, in our serving; the one who teaches, in his teaching; the one who exhorts, in his exhortation; the one who contributes, in generosity; the one who leads, with zeal; the one who does acts of mercy, with cheerfulness.
ROMANS 12:6–8

We all have different things we're good at, and God expects us to use those gifts for Him. But that doesn't excuse us from exercising *all* the gifts or developing *all* the fruits of the Spirit. Some people are givers. They are naturally generous and find joy in sharing what they have. Still, the rest of us have an obligation to give. Some are compassionate by nature. But each of us is called to show compassion to those who are hurting.

Our gifts tell us what we're good at. They give us direction for where and how we might best serve God. But we're all commanded to love, which means as much as possible, we strive to take on every facet of God's character so others can know Him too.

Father, show me where my gifts lie. Make it clear where and how You'd like me to serve You and others. But also develop the parts of me that are weak. When others look at me, I want them to see You.

BECOMING LIKE GOD

Let love be genuine. Abhor what is evil; hold fast to what is good. Love one another with brotherly affection. Outdo one another in showing honor. Do not be slothful in zeal, be fervent in spirit, serve the Lord. Rejoice in hope, be patient in tribulation, be constant in prayer. Contribute to the needs of the saints and seek to show hospitality.
ROMANS 12:9–13

This list of dos and don'ts provides a practical gauge for godly living. At any time, we can compare our words, thoughts, and actions to this inventory to measure how we're doing. Though we don't earn our place in heaven through our actions, the opposite is true. Our place in heaven—our relationship with God—should change our character. The more time we spend with Him, and the more we try to please Him, the more like Him we become.

God's love is genuine—there's nothing fake about it—so ours should be too. God hates evil, and so should we. God lifts us up, so we should lift each other up. When you read this index of godly traits, which areas do you notice need work? Tell Him you want to improve in those areas and ask Him to help you. He loves when we sincerely want to be like Him.

I'm so glad You never give up on me, Father. You know all my strengths and weaknesses. Make me more like You each day.

LOVE LIKE HE LOVES

Bless those who persecute you; bless and do not curse them. Rejoice with those who rejoice, weep with those who weep. Live in harmony with one another. Do not be haughty, but associate with the lowly. Never be wise in your own sight.

ROMANS 12:14–16

When Jesus hung on the cross, dying a death He didn't deserve, He said, "Father, forgive them, for they don't know what they are doing" (Luke 23:34 NLT). The crowds jeered, taunted, and mocked Him. . .and He blessed them. How is that humanly possible?

It's possible because of *love*. Too often we think of love as a feeling we act on. A more accurate way to think of love is as an action we choose, even when it's hard. It's the choice to bless others when they curse us, to show kindness when they are mean, to be generous when they are stingy. Love also means celebrating with others when they're happy, even if you've had a bad day. It means crying with someone who is sad or just sitting quietly with them so they know they're not alone. It means having lunch with the socially awkward person no one else wants to hang around with. And it means being humble, even when you think you have reason to gloat.

God is love, and we're called to be like Him. How can you show love today?

Your kind of love doesn't come naturally for me, Father. Teach me to love like You.

GOD'S JOB, MY JOB

Repay no one evil for evil, but give thought to do what is honorable in the sight of all. If possible, so far as it depends on you, live peaceably with all. Beloved, never avenge yourselves, but leave it to the wrath of God, for it is written, "Vengeance is mine, I will repay, says the Lord."
ROMANS 12:17–19

Have you ever been hurt so badly you wanted revenge? We all have. Or maybe someone you love was hurt and you want to take vengeance. You want to even the score. But that kind of attitude leads us down a muddy slope to anger, bitterness, and a miserable existence. God doesn't want His children playing on that particular field.

But you can be certain God sees. He is a just God, and He will punish all wrongs. He will bring justice much more thoroughly than we ever could. He wants us to keep doing the right thing, showing kindness, living peacefully, and displaying love. He doesn't want us to get our hands dirty. More importantly, He doesn't want His children to get hurt trying to play God.

When we've been injured or offended, it's hard to let God handle things. But He does His job much better than we can. We need to stick to our job, which is to love.

Loving others is hard when they've hurt me or someone I love, Lord. But You know this, don't You? I trust You to do Your job. Help me to do mine.

AGAINST HUMAN NATURE

To the contrary, "if your enemy is hungry, feed him; if he is thirsty, give him something to drink; for by so doing you will heap burning coals on his head." Do not be overcome by evil, but overcome evil with good.

ROMANS 12:20–21

These instructions for how to treat an enemy don't make any human sense. An enemy is someone who means you harm. Wouldn't it make more sense to fight them? To trip them up? To hurt them the same way they hurt you?

But God's way of getting vengeance goes against human reasoning. In 1 Corinthians 13, we're told that love never fails. God is love, and God is the most powerful one in the universe. When love meets hate, love always wins.

This kind of love isn't a weak, doormat kind of love. It's a force that stands tall, looks the enemy in the eye, and says, "I'm stronger than you are. I will respond, not react." And when that response is love, it brings shame and sorrow and repentance—sometimes. Even if it doesn't, love still wins, every single time.

Father, I've been so hurt. My human nature wants to hate, to wound, to retaliate. It's hard to love someone who's caused so much pain. But I know Your ways are better and higher than my ways. I'll trust You on this. Give me the strength to love.

SIN NATURE

The night is far gone; the day is at hand. So then let us cast off the works of darkness and put on the armor of light. Let us walk properly as in the daytime, not in orgies and drunkenness, not in sexual immorality and sensuality, not in quarreling and jealousy. But put on the Lord Jesus Christ, and make no provision for the flesh, to gratify its desires.
ROMANS 13:12–14

Before we knew Christ, we were controlled by our sinful natures. Even though we may have tried to be good people, there was a constant battle in our hearts and minds. We were tempted to lie or judge others harshly or cheat or do whatever else our nature wanted us to do.

When we invite Christ into our lives, there's not an automatic change. Instead, the more of Christ we seek, the more of God's Word we pour into our lives, the more we're transformed into His image. But that sin nature hangs around, like a pesky, barking Chihuahua. The difference is that previously, our sin nature had more power. We now have the Holy Spirit living in us. We have access to God's strength and authority. We don't have to listen to that barking dog, and we certainly don't have to obey it. Sin no longer controls us. We've given control of our lives to the Holy Spirit, and we can make the right choices as He empowers us.

Father, sometimes I feel my old sin nature pulling on me. Remind me of Your strength. When I'm weak, send me the help I need to stand against sin. I trust Your power in me.

DON'T JUDGE

Who are you to pass judgment on the servant of another? It is before his own master that he stands or falls. And he will be upheld, for the Lord is able to make him stand.
ROMANS 14:4

God tells us in His Word not to judge others. But that doesn't mean we must ignore the plain, black-and-white commands given in the Bible. He's made it clear that murder is wrong, so when we punish someone for murder, we're simply agreeing with a judgment God has already made.

But there are many gray areas that we're supposed to leave between the person and God. For example, some Christians believe it's best to abstain from alcoholic beverages completely, because they don't want to lose control and say or do something they'll regret. Others believe it's fine to drink alcohol in moderation, as long as they don't get drunk. The Bible doesn't give a clear mandate about this—it says not to get drunk with wine, but Jesus turned water into wine at a wedding. So it would be wrong of us to judge someone who's made a different choice about alcohol than we have. We also don't know all the circumstances that have led a person to their current position or circumstance. Those gray areas—the ones that don't break any law and aren't addressed specifically in God's Word—are to be left to God to judge. He sees what we cannot. He sees people's hearts.

Lord, I'm sorry for judging others. Remind me to love them and leave the judging to You.

DIFFERENCES IN FAITH

The faith that you have, keep between yourself and God. Blessed is the one who has no reason to pass judgment on himself for what he approves. But whoever has doubts is condemned if he eats, because the eating is not from faith. For whatever does not proceed from faith is sin.
ROMANS 14:22–23

At first glance, this verse can be confusing. We're supposed to share our faith! Why does Paul tell us to keep it to ourselves? But he's not referring to our faith in Christ. In context, he's talking about the belief that we can make some decisions for ourselves, even if they're different from others' beliefs. Specifically, the Jewish Christians had been brought up to believe it was wrong to consume certain kinds of meat, such as pork. The Gentile Christians held no such belief.

Paul didn't want these issues to become divisive. There is freedom in Christ. But if we know something might offend or cause others to doubt their own beliefs, we shouldn't make a big deal out of it.

If we feel strongly about something that's not clearly addressed in scripture, we should act on our own convictions. That's acting on our faith. If we think something is wrong and do it anyway, it's sin. But we shouldn't judge others for making different choices. Remember, God sees our intent, because He sees our hearts.

Father, thank You for giving us freedom and for making us all unique. I want to honor You in all my choices.

ABOUND

*May the God of hope fill you with all joy and peace in believing,
so that by the power of the Holy Spirit you may abound in hope.*
ROMANS 15:13

Did you know hope is the opposite of fear? Fear is the belief that something bad will happen. Hope is the belief that good things are in store. Paul reminds us that our God is the God of hope. He is love, and all His ways come from that love. Every good and perfect gift is from Him (James 1:17).

This prayer, that the God of hope will fill us with joy and peace, is a beautiful thought. It's also a reality. Paul simply agrees with God that these blessings already belong to us. When we lack peace, we can call on the Holy Spirit who lives in us, and He will give us peace. When joy eludes us, we can ask the Holy Spirit to make us joyful. The joy is already there. We just must access it by drawing near to God and letting His Spirit abound in us.

The word *abound* means to be filled to overflowing. When His Spirit abounds in us, we have the hope, joy, and peace that come only from God. The more time we spend in God's Word and in prayer, and the more we long to please Him, the more abundant His Spirit becomes in our lives.

**Heavenly Father, thank You for giving me hope, joy,
and peace. I want Your Spirit to abound in me.**

WISE AND INNOCENT

For your obedience is known to all, so that I rejoice over you, but I want you to be wise as to what is good and innocent as to what is evil.

ROMANS 16:19

Some may encourage Christians to take part in worldly practices for the sake of knowing what's it's like or being able to relate to people in that world. But there's never any good reason for a Christian to sin willingly. The idea that "innocent" means naive or gullible is a myth. Innocence and wisdom coexist. We don't have to be worldly to be wise, for wisdom comes from God.

Someone who doesn't know the truth may not recognize a lie. But to the one who knows the truth, lies are obvious. We don't have to try out worldly ways to see if there's some merit to them. We already know.

Because wisdom comes from God, we become wise by spending time with Him through prayer and the study of His Word. The more we seek Him, the more He makes Himself known to us. And the closer we are to God, the greater the contrast when we see evil. Wisdom helps us avoid evil and keeps us innocent.

Forgive me for inviting sin into my mind, thoughts, and practices. I know I won't find wisdom by experiencing a sinful, evil world. I want to be wise as to what is good and innocent as to what is evil.

THE COMPARISON TRAP

For consider your calling, brothers: not many of you were wise according to worldly standards, not many were powerful, not many were of noble birth. But God chose what is foolish in the world to shame the wise; God chose what is weak in the world to shame the strong.
1 CORINTHIANS 1:26–27

For all its benefits, social media is one of the greatest pitfalls of mental health in history. We all post and share the good parts of our lives. We use filters to present a beautiful, yet false, reality. And then we compare our real lives to the fake ones we see others share.

There are no winners in the comparison game. We may feel beautiful today, but tomorrow we'll see someone more beautiful. We may feel good about our home until we see an old friend share a picture of their more expensive home. There will always be someone smarter, richer, more talented, more educated, more powerful.

The good news is that God isn't interested in our beauty or talent, money or abilities. He doesn't need anything from us. Don't ever worry that you're not good enough! To God, lack of intelligence or finances or power is a good thing—especially when accompanied by humility. God doesn't want us to try to compete with His glory. Instead, He wants to be glorified in us.

Father, I'm weak. Use my weakness to show off Your strength.

TALK ABOUT IT

And I, when I came to you, brothers, did not come proclaiming to you the testimony of God with lofty speech or wisdom. For I decided to know nothing among you except Jesus Christ and him crucified.

1 Corinthians 2:1–2

Anyone can share Christ with others. It doesn't take a lofty degree or a large social media platform. All we have to do is share our stories! Tell the people around you what Christ has done in your life. The simplicity of the message is what makes it appealing.

If you're nervous about sharing your faith, you're not alone. Many worry about how to open up those conversations. Ask God to give you the right words at the right time, and He will. We all have a story to tell, and we're all pretty good about talking about what's happened to us. Even Paul, one of the most educated men of his time, disregarded all his fancy learning and simply shared his experience, along with the wisdom he gained from seeking God.

What's your story? How has God made a difference for you? Look for people who need what God has given you, and share how His good news has changed your life.

I guess I make sharing Your love harder than it needs to be, Lord. Help me share my story with those who need to hear it. Give me the words to say at the right time.

THE PLAN

Or do you not know that the unrighteous will not inherit the kingdom of God? Do not be deceived: neither the sexually immoral, nor idolaters, nor adulterers, nor men who practice homosexuality, nor thieves, nor the greedy, nor drunkards, nor revilers, nor swindlers will inherit the kingdom of God. And such were some of you. But you were washed, you were sanctified, you were justified in the name of the Lord Jesus Christ and by the Spirit of our God.

1 Corinthians 6:9–11

These verses contain all the hope of salvation in such a short space. Sinners don't go to heaven. Period. God will not tolerate sin, because it destroys His children. No one with sin on their record will enter God's presence. If that were the end of the story, we'd all be doomed, because we've all sinned.

But wait! There's more. Because God loves us so much, and because He knew we were destined to eternal death, He came up with a plan. He sent His Son to remove our wrongs from the chart. Jesus took our sin, wiped it from our record, and moved it to His own life. He paid the penalty so we wouldn't have to.

What shameful thing is in your past? We all have something. Hold your head high, knowing that God doesn't associate that sin with you anymore. Through Christ, your record is clean.

Jesus, I can't thank You enough for what You did for me on the cross. I want the rest of my life to be lived in gratitude to You.

STAY FOCUSED

Do you not know that in a race all the runners run, but only one receives the prize? So run that you may obtain it. Every athlete exercises self-control in all things. They do it to receive a perishable wreath, but we an imperishable. So I do not run aimlessly; I do not box as one beating the air. But I discipline my body and keep it under control, lest after preaching to others I myself should be disqualified.
1 CORINTHIANS 9:24–27

During biblical times, athletic competitions were a prominent part of Greek culture. As a matter of fact, the Greeks held many of the same competitions we still enjoy watching in the modern Olympics, such as running, wrestling, jumping, javelin throwing, discus throwing, and boxing. The winner received a crown of celery leaves. There was no prize for second place.

Paul uses many athletic analogies in his writing because the people of that time would have understood the comparisons. Each race had many competitors, all of whom were among the best in their sport. But only one person could win—there was no room for error. If someone got distracted or looked at what others were doing, they'd fall behind. The winner was someone who kept their eyes on the prize.

Paul wants us to focus on the prize. While this life holds many blessings, our true prize will be awarded when we stand face-to-face with God.

I know my ultimate reward isn't just some hazy hope. It's a very real prize in a very real eternity. Help me stay focused on You, Father.

THE SEED

So is it with the resurrection of the dead. What is sown is perishable; what is raised is imperishable. It is sown in dishonor; it is raised in glory. It is sown in weakness; it is raised in power. It is sown a natural body; it is raised a spiritual body. If there is a natural body, there is also a spiritual body.
1 CORINTHIANS 15:42–44

Because many people in Bible times were agricultural, Paul knew they'd understand the life cycle of a seed. The seed itself contains life inside it, but it must be buried in the ground and nourished. Before the new life can break through, the seed has to die. It's just a husk. When that happens, if the seed has been nourished and has grown strong roots, its real purpose comes to life, bursting through the dirt to become tall and green and strong. But if the seed isn't properly nourished, it could remain dormant and die without producing anything.

We often focus too much on what happens this side of heaven. After all, it's the only life we know. But this body we live and breathe and feel and love in. . .it's just our seed. It's our husk. One day, each of our bodies will die. What happens then depends on our choices now. We can live for ourselves, but that won't nourish our souls. Or we can choose to live in faith, which will provide the nourishment and roots needed for eternal life.

I want to grow strong in my faith, Father. Water me. Nourish me. Prepare me to live out my purpose.

IMITATE GOD

Let all that you do be done in love.
1 Corinthians 16:14

Much of Paul's ministry took place as he traveled around sharing the good news of Jesus Christ. When he left a place, he continued ministering to those people through letters. These were often lengthy, because there were no Zoom meetings or smartphones to connect people. As Paul drew near the end of a letter, he'd often sum up the most important parts of his message or give final instructions.

This verse was part of Paul's final instructions to the Corinthians. It remains important for us today, as our main purpose on this earth is to love God and love others. Everything we do should fulfill that purpose.

None of us live out our purpose perfectly, because we're not God. But in his letter to the Ephesians (5:1), Paul said to be imitators of God as dearly loved children. Just as a small child imitates his or her parent, we are to imitate God. . .and God is love. All His actions are born of love, and ours should be too.

Have you failed to show love? Apologize, and see if you can make it right. Is God prompting you to show love in a certain way? Act on His direction. Speak softly. Be kind. Show generosity and compassion, mercy and grace.

I haven't always acted in love, Father. I'm sorry for that. Fill me with Your thoughts, Your compassion, and Your love. I want to be like You.

REFRESH

I rejoice at the coming of Stephanas and Fortunatus and Achaicus, because they have made up for your absence, for they refreshed my spirit as well as yours. Give recognition to such people.
1 Corinthians 16:17–18

According to Dictionary.com, the word *refresh* means "to provide new vigor and energy"; "to make fresh again. . .or cheer." Spending time with God by praying and reading His Word refreshes our spirits. But have you noticed there are certain people who make you smile and lift your heart? That's what these three men did for Paul.

It's important to look for people who refresh you. Life is hard enough without getting sucked into relationships with toxic people. It's even more important to be a refreshing kind of person. When we lift others up, encourage their spirits, and bring a bit of joy to their hearts, we take on the character of God.

Make it a practice to look others in the eye, smile, and call them by name. When possible, offer them a kind word. Show appreciation for their special gifts and talents. Compliment their character. Ask God to make you a conduit of His love, compassion, and grace. All these things are like water to a dry soul.

So many people suffer from anxiety, depression, and an overall dryness of spirit, Lord—sometimes even me. Refresh my soul. Send friends who will lift me up. And pour out Your love through my words and actions so I can refresh others.

FREEDOM

It is not that we think we are qualified to do anything on our own. Our qualification comes from God. He has enabled us to be ministers of his new covenant. This is a covenant not of written laws, but of the Spirit. The old written covenant ends in death; but under the new covenant, the Spirit gives life. . . . For the Lord is the Spirit, and wherever the Spirit of the Lord is, there is freedom.

2 Corinthians 3:5–6, 17 NLT

Before meeting Christ, Paul (then Saul) followed the letter of the law. He was educated in the Old Testament scriptures. He did everything the law required. Yet no matter what he did or how perfectly he did it, he was still sinful. That's why he says, "The old written covenant ends in death." Trying to earn salvation by perfectly following God's rules is pointless. Those rules do the opposite—they show us how flawed we are. We'll never measure up.

But Christ set us free from all that! He paid the price, made the sacrifice, and cleared our records. We don't have to be legalistic anymore. He doesn't judge us based on our strict adherence to a set of rules. When we accept Christ, God sees "Paid in Full" beside our names. The account has been settled.

We now serve Him freely—not from fear that we'll mess up but from gratitude for what He's done. That kind of service brings joy, fulfillment, and purpose.

**Thank You for setting me free, Lord.
I serve You willingly and with a grateful heart.**

THE CHOICE

"Therefore, come out from among unbelievers, and separate yourselves from them, says the Lord. Don't touch their filthy things, and I will welcome you. And I will be your Father, and you will be my sons and daughters, says the Lord Almighty."

2 Corinthians 6:17–18 nlt

The second half of this passage contains such beautiful promises, don't you think? God Himself will welcome us into His family and His home. He will be our Father. We will be His sons and daughters, with full rights of inheritance. That's pretty amazing.

But the promises rest on our compliance with the first part. We must separate ourselves from the world—mentally, physically, emotionally, and spiritually. He knows we're human and we must live in this world. He knows we'll still have contact with earthly things. But we don't have to immerse ourselves in the things of this world. As much as is humanly possible, He wants us to guard our hearts and minds, because everything we think and say and do flows from what we let in (Proverbs 4:23).

We can choose to live for the moment, plunging into sin and temporary pleasure, or we can choose to set ourselves apart as God's children. We can't have both—the choice is ours.

I choose You, Lord. It seems like an obvious choice, but sometimes, in the moment, I'm overwhelmed by what I want right here and now. Help me view life with an eternal perspective. More than anything, I choose You.

THE MULTIPLIER

Remember this: Whoever sows sparingly will also reap sparingly, and whoever sows generously will also reap generously. Each of you should give what you have decided in your heart to give, not reluctantly or under compulsion, for God loves a cheerful giver.
2 CORINTHIANS 9:6–7 NIV

God is a multiplier. He takes what we give Him and turns it into so much more. This is beautifully illustrated in John 6:8–13 with the story of the little boy with two fish and five barley loaves. Jesus took that little bit of food, multiplied it, and fed five thousand people. They ate until they were full, and the disciples had twelve basketfuls of food left over. Talk about a miracle!

He still works those kinds of miracles today. God knows that generosity is one of the keys to joy. He doesn't need our stuff. He's God. He owns it all, anyway. He has no interest in what we give out of guilt or a bad attitude. But when we're excited to give what we have, whether it's a little or a lot, He will multiply it—for both the giver and the recipient.

He may multiply through a raise or a better job, or through a deep discount for a needed item. He may multiply through healed relationships or new friendships. The principle is clear: God loves when we give with joy.

I'm sorry for being stingy with my resources, Lord. Teach me to give generously and with a cheerful heart.

BRAGGING RIGHTS

*But, "Let the one who boasts boast in the Lord."
For it is not the one who commends himself who is
approved, but the one whom the Lord commends.*

2 CORINTHIANS 10:17–18 NIV

As the early church spread, some teachers got caught up in who had the bigger following. Paul—an excellent writer—was apparently boring in person. So these other teachers began to boast about their skills and qualifications in an effort to one-up Paul. Sounds immature, but we still get sucked into this kind of nonsense today. Our heads are turned by those with exciting leadership styles and impressive résumés. But those things do little to reflect a person's heart.

To make his point, Paul references Jeremiah 9:24 (ESV), which says, "But let him who boasts boast in this, that he understands and knows me, that I am the LORD who practices steadfast love, justice, and righteousness in the earth. For in these things I delight, declares the LORD."

Our gifts, talents, and abilities come from God. Our opportunities for education and advancement also come from God. Rather than boasting about what we've accomplished, we should boast about how great our Father is, give Him credit, and point any spotlight to Him. This is called humility, and it's one of God's favorite traits in His children.

**Father, let me boast only in You
and in what You've done in my life.**

FAMILY

Finally, brothers and sisters, rejoice! Strive for full restoration, encourage one another, be of one mind, live in peace. And the God of love and peace will be with you.
2 Corinthians 13:11 niv

Christians form a family, and families don't always get along. They don't always agree. But when all is said and done, a strong, healthy family will be there for each other.

The Corinthian church had some issues, and they fought sometimes. Paul reminds them that they are family and urges them to restore their relationships with God and each other. Not much has changed in the last two thousand years. We still have trouble getting along.

What needs to happen for you to restore relationships with your Christian brothers and sisters? First, encourage one another. Too often we tear each other down, but it's hard to stay mad at someone who lifts you up. Next, be of one mind. That doesn't mean we all turn into robots with the same thoughts and ideas. Rather, God wants us to agree on the important stuff and focus on that. Don't get distracted by the petty things that don't really matter.

Finally, live in peace. Romans 12:18 tells us that as much as it depends on us, we should live at peace with everyone. This doesn't just mean people outside the church. It's perhaps even more important to live at peace with our spiritual family. If not, Satan will use us to destroy the church from the inside out.

Encourage each other. Be of one mind. Live in peace.

Father, help me set aside my pride and truly love my Christian family.

HOW TO WIN THE WAR

So I say, walk by the Spirit, and you will not gratify the desires of the flesh. For the flesh desires what is contrary to the Spirit, and the Spirit what is contrary to the flesh. They are in conflict with each other, so that you are not to do whatever you want.
GALATIANS 5:16–17 NIV

Humans are flawed, sinful creatures. That doesn't change when we accept Christ. We still walk around in the flesh, which means we'll still be tempted to do the things we've always done. But now we have the Holy Spirit living in us, which means the Spirit is at war with the flesh.

So how do we win that war? We do it by walking by the Spirit. When we walk with someone, we spend time with them. The more time we spend with that person, the better we know them. When we walk with the Holy Spirit, His power increases in us, and we're able to refuse temptation.

There's a constant battle going on within us. The side that will win is the side we pay the most attention to, the side we focus on and feed and energize. Walk by the Spirit. Hold His hand. Talk to Him, and fill your mind with His wisdom. Do those things, and He will do the rest.

I want to walk with You today and every day, Lord.

FRUITS AND ROOTS

But the fruit of the Spirit is love, joy, peace, patience, kindness, goodness, faithfulness, gentleness, self-control; against such things there is no law.
GALATIANS 5:22–23

This is a lovely, visual verse. It brings to mind a basket of bright, healthy fruit, juicy and ready to be eaten. Many people read this passage and focus on the fruit instead of the roots. But if a plant doesn't have healthy, strong roots, it won't produce delicious fruit.

The same is true in our lives. We won't become loving by trying to be loving any more than an apple core will grow into a tree with no soil or water. That tree must be in the right environment to grow and produce fruit. We become loving by spending time with our Father and growing more like Him. We may choose to do something kind every now and then, but kindness won't become a part of our character without a strong, daily bond with the Holy Spirit.

This list contains the fruit of the *Spirit*. That means the *Spirit* produces the fruit. We can't produce it on our own. If we want more fruit in our lives, or if we want healthier fruit, we must walk daily with the Holy Spirit.

I want the fruit of Your Holy Spirit to be abundant in my life, Lord. Walk with me each moment. I want to know You more.

SATURATED IN LOVE

*That Christ may dwell in your hearts through faith.
And I pray that you, being rooted and established in love,
may have power, together with all the Lord's holy people,
to grasp how wide and long and high and deep is the love of
Christ, and to know this love that surpasses knowledge—
that you may be filled to the measure of all the fullness of God.*
Ephesians 3:17–19 niv

This passage gets to the root of the Christian faith. It's not about religion and rules. It's about love! Specifically, it's about the incomprehensible, indescribable love of God for us.

Many of Paul's readers were familiar with the Pharisees—Jewish religious leaders who followed all the rules but did it without love (Luke 11:42). Paul wanted us to know that God isn't impressed by legalistic rule-followers. He is love, and He wants that love to live in us.

It's a love so big, our human minds can never comprehend it on our own. Only through God's power in us can we come close to understanding His love. Paul uses every measurable dimension known to man at that time—width, length, height, and depth—to describe God's vast, immeasurable love for us. Though we'll never fully grasp its magnitude, we should try. For in the trying, we soak in that love, allowing it to saturate our thoughts and hearts and actions until it pours out to others.

Help me understand Your love, Father. Make it come alive in me.

HIS POWER IN US

Now to him who is able to do immeasurably more than all we ask or imagine, according to his power that is at work within us, to him be glory in the church and in Christ Jesus throughout all generations, for ever and ever! Amen.
EPHESIANS 3:20–21 NIV

Many Christians focus on God's blessings. It's wonderful to practice gratitude for God's good gifts—it keeps us humble. But it's easy to spend time praying for *blessings* while forgetting about God's *power*. The key to a victorious Christian life is God's power in us.

Why do we try to do most things on our own, while waiting for a disaster before praying for God's power? His power lives in us all the time. Why do we choose to live mediocre lives when He can do "immeasurably more than all we ask or imagine, according to his power that is at work within us"?

His power ignites in us when we live our lives for His glory. It explodes and multiplies as we know Him more. That power isn't for our own glory or for pleasure or riches. He won't allow it. But when we truly give up our will for His, He starts showing off.

**Thank You for Your power in me, Lord.
My life is Yours to use as You please.**

THE LONG WALK

I therefore, a prisoner for the Lord, urge you to walk in a manner worthy of the calling to which you have been called, with all humility and gentleness, with patience, bearing with one another in love, eager to maintain the unity of the Spirit in the bond of peace.
EPHESIANS 4:1–3

During this time in history, walking was the most common mode of transportation. There were no trains or planes or automobiles. Few had access to chariots. Horses were used for battle, but they weren't commonly used for daily transportation. If a family owned a horse, it was most likely for plowing the fields or carrying heavy packs as the owner walked alongside.

When Paul urged his readers to walk in a worthy manner, he was really saying, "Travel through life in a way that honors God." The idea focuses on one step at a time, rather than the entire journey. Because we're used to getting places quickly, with cars or airplanes, it would be easy to miss the detail here. We don't develop godly traits that fast. Rather, they emerge slowly, one step at a time, small choice by small choice, as we seek to walk close to our Father and please Him in all we do.

I want to walk in a manner worthy of bearing Your name, Father. Help me focus on the small choices, repeated over time, that please You.

GET TO WORK!

So Christ himself gave the apostles, the prophets, the evangelists, the pastors and teachers, to equip his people for works of service, so that the body of Christ may be built up until we all reach unity in the faith and in the knowledge of the Son of God and become mature, attaining to the whole measure of the fullness of Christ.
EPHESIANS 4:11–13 NIV

Perhaps one of the biggest misunderstandings among modern Christians is the idea that those in full-time ministry are the ministers. When someone dies, we call the preacher. When a person needs food or comfort or guidance, we alert the pastor. But that's not biblically accurate. God appoints certain people to be in ministry "to equip His people for works of service, so that the body of Christ may be built up." It's not the minister's job to feed the hungry or visit the sick or disciple the wayward teen. It's *our* job.

Those with the formal title are tasked with preparing the rest of us to do our jobs. A good comparison might be a military commander. When there's a war, the troops don't call their commander and say, "Go fight!" It works the other way around. The commander prepares his troops for battle, and they do the fighting. The commander may fight alongside them, but he doesn't fight *instead* of them.

How ready are you to do God's work? Reach out to your spiritual leader for help with preparation. Then lace up your combat boots and get to work.

Prepare me to do the work You've called me to do, Lord.

A BROKEN HEART

And do not grieve the Holy Spirit of God, with whom you were sealed for the day of redemption. Get rid of all bitterness, rage and anger, brawling and slander, along with every form of malice. Be kind and compassionate to one another, forgiving each other, just as in Christ God forgave you.
EPHESIANS 4:30–32 NIV

If you've ever lost a loved one, you know what grief feels like. It's a deep, sinking, foggy feeling that's hard to navigate. Watching people you love fight with each other is another form of grief. When God—whose character is love—watches His children destroy each other with anger and gossip and slander and fighting and meanness, He is *grieved*. The Holy Spirit's heart is broken.

Just the thought of breaking the Spirit's heart is shameful. But that's what we do each time we respond to each other in a hurtful way. Unfortunately, Christians often have a reputation for being unkind and harsh and judgmental with each other, as well as with those outside the church. When we act that way, outsiders don't want to have anything to do with us. Satan has a party when we bicker and fight with our Christian brothers and sisters. He doesn't have to destroy our reputation. We do a fine job of that on our own.

Yet all of this could be avoided by choosing to be kind. Compassionate. Patient. Forgiving. After all, that's how Christ treats us.

**I'm sorry for ever causing You grief, Lord.
Teach me to love others the way You love me.**

STAND

Finally, be strong in the Lord and in his mighty power. Put on the full armor of God, so that you can take your stand against the devil's schemes. For our struggle is not against flesh and blood, but against the rulers, against the authorities, against the powers of this dark world and against the spiritual forces of evil in the heavenly realms. Therefore put on the full armor of God, so that when the day of evil comes, you may be able to stand your ground, and after you have done everything, to stand.
Ephesians 6:10–13 niv

In a boxing match, the opponents go at each other. They hit and punch and fight with all they've got. They wear protective gear, but sometimes they still get hurt. A few rounds in, they're bloody and bruised and exhausted. They may even fall down, but they get back up. . .until they can't get up anymore. The winner is the one left standing.

With all that's going on in our world, it's important to be armed and ready to fight. We're in a spiritual battle, and we *will* get hurt. At times, we'll feel bloody and bruised. At times, we'll fall down. But with God's armor, described in Ephesians 6, we'll always get back up. At the end of it all, we will stand victorious.

Thank You for the protective gear of salvation, righteousness, truth, peace, faith, and Your Word. Help me always remember to wear my full armor.

HOMESICK

If I am to go on living in the body, this will mean fruitful labor for me. Yet what shall I choose? I do not know! I am torn between the two: I desire to depart and be with Christ, which is better by far; but it is more necessary for you that I remain in the body.
PHILIPPIANS 1:22–24 NIV

A 1976 song by singer/songwriter B. J. Thomas, titled "Home Where I Belong" communicates that heaven and earth are both lovely, but if we had only one choice, we'd choose heaven. Because heaven is "home"—the place where we belong. The song's lyrics echo Peter's words in 1 Peter 2:11 (NASB), where he says that as God's people, we're "foreigners and strangers" in this world. It's not unusual for Christians to feel homesick for a place we've never been.

Yet we have work to do while we're here. God planned you before you were born; gave you your personality, your gifts, and your talents; and placed you in this exact time and place so you could do His will. He has perfectly equipped you to do whatever He calls you to. One day you'll be home, and won't that be great? In the meantime, there is much to do.

This world makes me weary sometimes, Lord. I look forward to the time when I can see You face-to-face. Until then, I'll do all I can to share Your love with those around me.

OUTWARD FOCUS

Do nothing out of selfish ambition or vain conceit. Rather, in humility value others above yourselves, not looking to your own interests but each of you to the interests of the others. In your relationships with one another, have the same mindset as Christ Jesus: who, being in very nature God, did not consider equality with God something to be used to his own advantage; rather, he made himself nothing by taking the very nature of a servant, being made in human likeness. And being found in appearance as a man, he humbled himself by becoming obedient to death—even death on a cross!
PHILIPPIANS 2:3–8 NIV

There's a mental health crisis going on in our world. More people than ever live with chronic depression, anxiety, and other disorders that make us feel sad and dissatisfied. God's mandate that we put others first isn't just a call to be servants. And He's certainly not encouraging us to be doormats with no boundaries, letting others use and abuse us.

But God's wisdom is far above our own human wisdom. Studies have shown what God has always told us. Focusing outward, serving others, is one of the best things we can do for our own mental health. When we look for others who are sad, hurting, or in need, and we try to make their lives better in some way, we are distracted from our own problems. By lifting others up, we get lifted up as well.

Thank You for focusing on my needs instead of Your own, Father. Show me how I can make someone else's life better.

LIKE CHRIST

I want to know Christ—yes, to know the power of his resurrection and participation in his sufferings, becoming like him in his death.
PHILIPPIANS 3:10 NIV

This prayer is contrary to everything in our human nature. Paul wants to suffer like Christ? That's crazy. No one wants to suffer!

But the focus here isn't on the suffering. It's on becoming like Christ. Paul already knew what it was to suffer for Christ. He'd been arrested, imprisoned, and shipwrecked. He'd experienced sickness and hunger, and at one point he didn't have a coat to keep him warm.

Through all this hardship, he learned to be like his Lord. He learned to be content in all circumstances. He learned to put others' needs before his own. He learned to focus on the bigger picture—winning others to Christ. Paul knew his reward would come in heaven.

When we face hardship, we can fuss and complain and ask, "Why?" Or we can recognize that hardship builds character, if we let it. We can rejoice even in our suffering, knowing that God wants to use our circumstances to draw us closer to Him and make us more like Him. The more like Him we become, the more we see His power at work in our lives.

I'm not enjoying my current circumstances, Lord. But I rejoice in them anyway. Use them to make me more like You.

THINK ABOUT THESE THINGS

Finally, brothers and sisters, whatever is true, whatever is noble, whatever is right, whatever is pure, whatever is lovely, whatever is admirable—if anything is excellent or praiseworthy—think about such things. Whatever you have learned or received or heard from me, or seen in me— put it into practice. And the God of peace will be with you.
PHILIPPIANS 4:8–9 NIV

According to the Mayo Clinic, there's one small change we can all make that has enormous positive effects on both mental and physical well-being. We can be thankful! When we make gratitude a daily practice, it takes our minds off what's wrong with our lives and places our focus on what's right. Thankfulness has been proven to improve symptoms of depression and anxiety, decrease stress, and even improve chronic pain. The lowered stress improves blood pressure and other health issues. We become happier, which helps us become more active. . . . Gratitude has a domino effect leading to all-around wellness.

If you're in the depths of despair, think of one thing you're grateful for. It may not improve things overnight, but this one daily practice, over time, will have an amazing impact on your attitude and health.

If you don't know where to start, you can begin with Paul's list. Whatever is true, noble, right, pure, lovely, and admirable—think about these things.

Thank You for loving me, Father. Thank You for Jesus. Thank You for making me Your child.

THE KEY TO HAPPINESS

I am not saying this because I am in need, for I have learned to be content whatever the circumstances. I know what it is to be in need, and I know what it is to have plenty. I have learned the secret of being content in any and every situation, whether well fed or hungry, whether living in plenty or in want. I can do all this through him who gives me strength.

PHILIPPIANS 4:11–13 NIV

The Harvard Study of Adult Development was the world's longest study on what it takes to be happy. Most of us are under the assumption that more money, better jobs, and fancier cars will bring happiness, but that isn't true. While those in severe poverty gain happiness when their basic needs are met, further material goods don't affect our happiness much at all. If anything, more stuff equals more stress.

Paul knew this secret long before the Harvard study. He had known what it was like to have plenty and what it was like to be in need. Whether in abundance or in want, inner joy can be achieved only through a close relationship with Jesus Christ. He gives us strength to face anything with confidence, contentment, and peace.

Thank You for giving me all the keys to happiness in my relationship with You, Lord.

FULLY DEVOTED

Devote yourselves to prayer, being watchful and thankful.
Colossians 4:2 niv

Have you ever devoted yourself to something? To devote means to dedicate or give up something in pursuit of a cause or goal. We might devote ourselves to getting healthy or devote our time to volunteering at an animal shelter. Devotion is a commitment to something because it's worthy and important.

Paul urges his readers to make prayer a priority. In other places, he refers to *earnest prayer*. This kind of prayer isn't a rote dinner blessing. Rather, it's having deep, sincere conversations with God. Paul also reminds us to be watchful—we should always look for how God is working. Even when we don't see evidence right away, we can be assured that God is actively bringing about His purpose in our lives. Finally, we're to be thankful, for a heart of gratitude pleases God.

What are you devoting yourself to? If you're volunteering for a good cause or you've committed to making positive changes, good for you! But don't forget to devote yourself to the most important things of all—a strong relationship with God. Commit yourself to prayer (time with God), look for evidence of His presence, and be grateful for all the ways He has blessed you and others.

I'm sorry for praying half-heartedly and for not fully committing myself to You, Lord. I want to devote myself completely to knowing You more.

ONE DAY

For the Lord himself will come down from heaven, with a loud command, with the voice of the archangel and with the trumpet call of God, and the dead in Christ will rise first. After that, we who are still alive and are left will be caught up together with them in the clouds to meet the Lord in the air. And so we will be with the Lord forever. Therefore encourage one another with these words.
1 Thessalonians 4:16–18 niv

This life has some beautiful moments for sure. Growing strong, finding a way to use your gifts and talents, falling in love, getting married, having children and grandchildren, helping others. . .those are just a few of the things that make our time here worth living. Yet the longer we live, the more we know that heartache, pain, and sorrow are also a part of life.

One day, Christians will join Christ! There will be no more suffering or pain (Revelation 21:3-4). We will have new, better bodies (1 Corinthians 15:35–44). We'll have a forever kind of joy (Psalm 16:11). We'll have a beautiful home prepared just for us (John 14:1-4). All the hard parts of life will disappear—no more bills or depression or car accidents or health problems or natural disasters. No more violence or crime. We will spend the rest of eternity in God's presence, delighting in Him as He pours out His love on us.

I can't wait to see You face-to-face, Lord.

GOD'S WILL FOR YOU

Rejoice always, pray continually, give thanks in all circumstances; for this is God's will for you in Christ Jesus.
1 Thessalonians 5:16–18 NIV

Have you ever wondered, *What is God's will for my life?* This verse answers that question. He created each of us with unique gifts, talents, and abilities. But rather than programming us like robots, He gives us a lot of free choice. He is all about freedom. Someone who is good at math could equally serve Him and help others by being an accountant, a teacher, an engineer, a stay-at-home parent, or even a doctor.

But no matter what path we take with our careers, no matter how we may use our uniqueness to serve God and others, He's clear about His main purpose for us: He wants a relationship with us.

Isn't that cool? He created us because He wanted us in His life.

Rejoice always—this makes God smile. Pray continually—He loves talking with you. Give thanks in all circumstances—this makes Him feel loved and appreciated. These practices connect us to our Father, and the more connected we are to Him, the better we're able to love others.

Sometimes I don't feel like rejoicing, Father. But I know joy isn't based on my circumstances—it's based on my future. Remind me to rejoice always, even in hard times. Remind me to stay connected to You through prayer. Thank You for loving me so much that You want a relationship with me. I'm so grateful.

TRUE CHILD IN FAITH

Paul, an apostle of Christ Jesus by command of God our Savior and of Christ Jesus our hope, to Timothy, my true child in the faith: grace, mercy, and peace from God the Father and Christ Jesus our Lord.

1 TIMOTHY 1:1–2

Paul's letters make up much of the New Testament. Most of his letters address large groups. He'd send a letter to the entire gathering of Christians in that place. Someone would read it aloud, and they'd use his words as a source of teaching and discussion.

Timothy is the only person we know of who received not one but two *personal* letters from Paul. He calls Timothy his "true child in the faith." He may have personally led Timothy to Christ. Or he may have just taken a special interest in discipling this young man.

God is all about relationships. We should make it a goal to have three types of friendships. First, befriend someone who is more spiritually mature than you are—someone you can look to for guidance and wisdom. Next, be friends with people who share your values and goals to be like Christ, who are at a similar place in their spiritual journey. Those are the people who hold you up when you stumble. . .and you do the same for them. Finally, try to be the Paul to someone's Timothy. Find someone who needs the wisdom you've gained from walking with Christ and help light the way for them.

Lead me to the godly, Christian relationships you want me to have, Lord. Help me as I help others on their spiritual journeys.

MONEY

For the love of money is a root of all kinds of evils. It is through this craving that some have wandered away from the faith and pierced themselves with many pangs. But as for you, O man of God, flee these things. Pursue righteousness, godliness, faith, love, steadfastness, gentleness.

1 Timothy 6:10–11

One of the easiest ways to lose your focus on God is to focus on money. Notice Paul didn't say *money* is the root of all kinds of evils. Money is just money. It's an inanimate object. It doesn't have a soul. If you put it in a locked box, it will never scratch or claw to fight its way out. Money is simply a tool, and used the right way, it can do a lot of good things.

If someone has a lot of money and they love people more than anything, they'll use that money to show love. If they have money and use it to support a cause they care about, that's great. But when anyone falls in love with money, it becomes like a cancer to the spirit. It leads to greed and materialism. If allowed to grow, the love of money will cause a breakdown of character. People lie and cheat and steal and kill, all for the love of this inanimate object.

The godly person should be warned against placing too much importance on money. Instead, pursue righteousness, godliness, faith, love, steadfastness (being solid and reliable), and gentleness. These qualities will pay much greater dividends, both here and in eternity.

**Help me pursue only worthy qualities, Lord.
Keep me from loving money too much.**

A GOOD FRIEND

May the Lord grant mercy to the household of Onesiphorus, for he often refreshed me and was not ashamed of my chains, but when he arrived in Rome he searched for me earnestly and found me—may the Lord grant him to find mercy from the Lord on that day!—and you well know all the service he rendered at Ephesus.
2 TIMOTHY 1:16–18

Paul wrote much of the New Testament while in prison. In addition to revealing Paul's passion for sharing Christ, the abundance of his writing may offer a clue that he was lonely. He had to do something with his time! His friend Onesiphorus went out of his way to find Paul, visit him, help provide for his needs, and just be a good friend. And it sounds like he took care of Paul more than once. . .he refreshed and served Paul often.

Being a loyal friend is so important. You never know when you may be the only person someone can count on. We all tend to paste smiles on our faces while going through our own private battles. Be the person who notices when someone hasn't shown up, when they're quieter than usual, when they just don't seem themselves. And if you know of their personal struggles, all the more reason to support them. Be the one who brightens someone's day when everything else around them is dark.

Too often I get caught up in my own private thoughts and forget to notice others' struggles, Lord. Teach me to be a good friend.

ROYAL

So flee youthful passions and pursue righteousness, faith, love, and peace, along with those who call on the Lord from a pure heart. Have nothing to do with foolish, ignorant controversies; you know that they breed quarrels. And the Lord's servant must not be quarrelsome but kind to everyone, able to teach, patiently enduring evil, correcting his opponents with gentleness. God may perhaps grant them repentance leading to a knowledge of the truth.

2 Timothy 2:22–25

If you've ever watched members of a royal family interact with the public, you've seen a standard of behavior that's different from the way the masses act. Royals stand up straight and hold up their chins. Their manners are impeccable. They often come across as gracious, humble, and kind. Royals avoid getting involved in petty, public squabbles. When royal teens are caught getting into mischief like many other teens, it's considered scandalous and shameful. Because of their status, they're held to a higher standard.

As God's children, we are part of His royal family. We're held to a higher standard than the rest of the world. When we get pulled into foolish behavior, we bring shame on our Father's name. We are royal, and He expects us to behave as such.

He knows we're not perfect, and He doesn't expect us to be. But He does want us to be disciplined and do our best to represent Him well.

Thank You for making me a part of Your royal family, Lord. Help me behave in a way that brings honor to Your name.

AVOID THEM

But understand this, that in the last days there will come times of difficulty. For people will be lovers of self, lovers of money, proud, arrogant, abusive, disobedient to their parents, ungrateful, unholy, heartless, unappeasable, slanderous, without self-control, brutal, not loving good, treacherous, reckless, swollen with conceit, lovers of pleasure rather than lovers of God, having the appearance of godliness, but denying its power. Avoid such people.

2 Timothy 3:1–5

It feels like we've been in the last days for a long time. Each generation seems to slip a little farther down the ravine. The last phrase in this passage, "having the appearance of godliness, but denying its power," is perhaps the most disturbing.

Our church pews are emptier than ever. Our young people are turning away from God because many of them don't see an authenticity in the way we practice our faith. Of those who do go to church, many of them are there for the social aspect—to make friends, to be around the "right" people, to see and be seen in the community.

Even those who don't claim a relationship with God may practice a "form of godliness" by championing causes that seem good on the surface but that don't honor God. In this second personal letter to Timothy, Paul warns against such people. He says to avoid them. No one is harder to win over to Christ than the person who already thinks he's righteous. Love people like this. Show them what God's kindness looks like. But don't let them become an intimate part of your life.

Father, thank You for Your warnings and for Your wisdom.

FINAL WORDS

*I have fought the good fight, I have finished the race,
I have kept the faith. Henceforth there is laid up for me
the crown of righteousness, which the Lord, the righteous
judge, will award to me on that day, and not only to
me but also to all who have loved his appearing.*

2 TIMOTHY 4:7–8

When Paul wrote these words, he knew his life would end soon. He'd spent a long time in a Roman prison. He'd stood before the judge, and he didn't expect another day in court. He was pretty sure he'd be executed before long.

Rather than fret about the unfairness of it all, he faced it with a smile. He said, "I've done what I came here to do." He served God to the best of his ability. He poured out his life to make sure others knew God loved them. His ministry, his service to God, was responsible for much of the spread of Christianity during the days of the early church.

At some point, each of us will live our last day on earth. It may be tomorrow or many years from now. But it should be our goal that when that day comes, we can say what Paul did: *I never gave up on my faith in God. I lived for Him the best I could. I served Him and loved Him and led others to Him.*

What a day that will be!

I make Paul's words my prayer, Lord. Help me
fight Your fight, finish the race You've laid out
for me, and never waver in my faith. I love You.

LONELY BUT NOT ALONE

At my first defense no one came to stand by me, but all deserted me. May it not be charged against them! But the Lord stood by me and strengthened me, so that through me the message might be fully proclaimed and all the Gentiles might hear it. So I was rescued from the lion's mouth. The Lord will rescue me from every evil deed and bring me safely into his heavenly kingdom. To him be the glory forever and ever. Amen.

2 TIMOTHY 4:16–18

After all Paul had done to spread the gospel and help establish the early church, he had to stand in court by himself. No one—not a single person—stood with him. They were probably afraid they would be executed too. Paul knew what it felt like to be truly alone.

Christ knew that feeling too. Most of His friends deserted Him as He stood trial and then was crucified. Only John and His mother stayed with Him at the cross.

When you feel lonely, remember you are not alone. Paul wrote, "The Lord stood by me and strengthened me." God will do the same for each of His children. Many times in His Word—too many to list here—He promises, "I will never leave you or forsake you." Lean into God. Sink into His presence. He loves you, and He will never leave you. No matter what happens or how dark things seem or how abandoned you may feel, *you are not alone.*

Thank You for never leaving me alone, Lord.

HE GETS IT

Therefore he had to be made like his brothers in every respect, so that he might become a merciful and faithful high priest in the service of God, to make propitiation for the sins of the people. For because he himself has suffered when tempted, he is able to help those who are being tempted.
HEBREWS 2:17–18

Around 10 percent of couples in the United States struggle with infertility. It's a heartbreaking issue that's often hard to put into words. While people around them may have compassion, it's a problem no one can truly understand unless they've been through it.

That's what Jesus did for us. The previous verse, Hebrews 2:16, refers to the angels, who aren't human and therefore don't experience heartache or temptation the way humans do. They see what's happening to us, but they're not much help in that area because they don't understand how we feel. Jesus, on the other hand, left His throne in heaven to become human. He experienced hunger, sickness, and heartache. He was tempted in every way known to man, but He didn't sin (Hebrews 4:14–16). He gets what we're going through, because He's been there.

When you feel overwhelmed, reach for Jesus. Get as close to Him as you possibly can. He will help you, comfort you, and lead you. He knows how you feel, and He will rescue you.

Sometimes I forget You truly understand how I feel, Jesus. Thank You for all You went through to rescue me. Let me feel Your presence as You lead me through this difficult time.

FAITH AND FRIENDS

Let us hold fast the confession of our hope without wavering, for he who promised is faithful. And let us consider how to stir up one another to love and good works, not neglecting to meet together, as is the habit of some, but encouraging one another, and all the more as you see the Day drawing near.
Hebrews 10:23–25

The book of Hebrews was written to Jewish Christians who were under fire. They suffered discrimination, and many of them considered going back to Judaism, which was more accepted. The author encourages them to hold fast to hope because God will not let them down. They're also reminded to encourage one another. There is strength in numbers. It's important to build relationships with other Christians so we can cheer each other on and hold each other up.

The Christian faith is not designed to be a solitary faith. God is all about relationships. That's why He created us—so He could know us and we could know Him. When we go rogue and wander off to live out our faith alone, we're more likely to give in to temptation. We all have bad days and weak moments, and if no one is around to hold us accountable, we're more likely to make poor choices.

Hold fast to your faith and your Christian friends. God is good, and so is being surrounded by people who share your love for Christ.

Father, lead me to Christian friends at work, in my neighborhood, and at my church. Thank You for the hope I find in You.

HANG IN THERE

Therefore do not throw away your confidence, which has a great reward. For you have need of endurance, so that when you have done the will of God you may receive what is promised.
HEBREWS 10:35–36

The message of the book of Hebrews is this: Don't throw away your faith in God and in His Son, Jesus Christ. Hang in there, because what you believe is the truth. One day your faith will reap a great reward.

The modern Christian has a lot in common with those early Jewish Christians. In many ways, we are rejected by society. We are mocked and shunned. Sometimes the discrimination is subtle; other times it's more obvious. But any Christian who has to live and work among non-Christians has felt the burn of rejection at some point.

But we know the truth. We have confidence that God is real, that Jesus Christ is His Son, and that His Word is true. Don't cut your faith loose to make your life easier in the short term. Hold fast. Endure. Don't throw away your relationship with the Holy Father, because enduring faith brings great reward—both now and in eternity.

I love You, Father. I love being a Christian—most of the time. But sometimes my faith wobbles, and I wonder if the discrimination and rejection are worth it. Sometimes I just want to be normal and accepted and liked. Teach me to endure, to hang in there with You, even when it's hard. You are worth it.

PRAISE GOD AND DO GOOD

Through him then let us continually offer up a sacrifice of praise to God, that is, the fruit of lips that acknowledge his name. Do not neglect to do good and to share what you have, for such sacrifices are pleasing to God. Obey your leaders and submit to them, for they are keeping watch over your souls, as those who will have to give an account. Let them do this with joy and not with groaning, for that would be of no advantage to you.
HEBREWS 13:15–17

As the author wraps up this letter to the Hebrews, three main reminders are given. First, praise God *all the time*. Psalm 22:3 tells us God inhabits the praises of His people. That means our praise is His physical address. He lives in our praise! If we ever want to feel His presence, if we want to bring Him closer, we can praise Him. He will be right there.

Next, do good and share what you have. We're put here to love others. We're blessed with material wealth so we can bless others. When we do this, we lift others' spirits, and our own spirits are lifted too.

Finally, work hard and obey your leaders. God puts leaders into place, and we can trust Him to call them to task when it's needed. Our job is to honor God by honoring our bosses and government leaders. God wants us to be above reproach in all things so that others will notice the difference He makes in our lives.

I praise You, Father. I want to honor You by blessing and honoring others.

SERVANT

James, a servant of God and of the Lord Jesus Christ.
JAMES 1:1

What does it mean to be a servant? It means someone else is the boss. Someone else is calling the shots. The servant's job is to do whatever the boss tells them to do. It would be impertinent to question the boss. The servant's job is simply to carry out orders.

As servants of God, what are our orders? Here's a short list:
- Love God with our whole hearts.
- Love others as we love ourselves, looking out for their needs as we would our own.
- Be humble. Put God first, others second, and ourselves last.
- Do good works to show God's love in this world.
- Work hard.
- Talk with God continually, including Him in all our thoughts, actions, and conversations.
- Trust God.
- Worship God. Praise God. Thank God.
- Keep loving.

While this isn't a comprehensive list, it covers the highlights. Like James, we are servants of God and of the Lord Jesus Christ. That means we answer to God alone. How blessed we are to serve such a loving, kind, gracious God!

Sometimes I treat You like my servant, Father. I tell You what I want, and I get frustrated when You don't respond to my wishes. I'm so sorry for my lack of humility! I am Your servant. I'll do whatever You tell me to do.

TAMING THE TONGUE

If anyone thinks he is religious and does not bridle his tongue but deceives his heart, this person's religion is worthless.
JAMES 1:26

James gets right to the point. We all have big mouths, and we all have trouble controlling our tongues. It's common to think a little gossip doesn't hurt—until you're the one being gossiped about. We need to stop viewing our words as harmless and recognize them as dangerous.

Our tongues are weapons. They wound hearts. They destroy lives. Sometimes they even kill. Most of us know better than to walk around with a loaded gun, randomly shooting into a crowd. If we did that, we'd go to prison for a very long time. Yet we aim and shoot our words with no consideration for who they wound. The damage is often permanent.

When we call ourselves Christians and we run off at the mouth, using no safety, no filter, James says we deceive ourselves. Christianity is about love.

Though none of us can perfectly control our tongues all the time (James 3:8), we can try. We do have free will, and we can do our best to speak only love, encouragement, and compassionate truth. God sees our hearts, and He knows when we're doing our best. He forgives our failures, but He doesn't tolerate outright rebellion and meanness. Next time you're tempted to say something unkind, say something loving instead, or remain quiet. The more you practice, the easier it gets.

Help me control my tongue, Lord. Remind me it's a weapon and to keep it on safety. I want my words to love and not wound.

TRUE RELIGION

Religion that is pure and undefiled before God the Father is this: to visit orphans and widows in their affliction, and to keep oneself unstained from the world.
JAMES 1:27

Visiting orphans and widows. . .that sounds like such a nice job. When we hear of others taking care of those who can't take care of themselves, we're filled with admiration. But call any church office and ask about the percentage of people who actually do it, and you'll discover it's very low. Visiting the elderly and shut-ins or reaching out to children in foster care is often relegated to once-a-year feel-good events, like singing Christmas carols at the nursing home or hiding Easter eggs for needy children. That's not what this verse means.

Religion—the formal, organizational set of beliefs and practices we observe as a way to show our faith—means nothing to God. It's our *actions* that impress Him. . .specifically, actions driven by love, kindness, and compassion.

God wants us to stay "unstained from the world." That means we have to set ourselves apart from things that don't please God. So what do we do with all that free time gained from saying no to worldly pleasures? We make an older person smile by bringing them a hot meal or wheeling their garbage to the street on trash day. We build relationships with children who have few, if any, positive role models in their lives. This pleases God. . .and it makes us feel pretty good too.

Show me people I can love, Lord. I want to please You.

A FRIEND OF GOD

*And the Scripture was fulfilled that says,
"Abraham believed God, and it was counted to him as
righteousness"—and he was called a friend of God.*
JAMES 2:23

How would you feel if a chance encounter with Prince William and Catherine, Princess of Wales, led to a close, enduring friendship with that couple? The thought of being in royalty's inner circle is thrilling. What an honor!

Yet William and Catherine's influence is limited to this time and place in history. God, the King of kings and Lord of lords, is eternal, all-powerful, and almighty. This verse tells us how to become part of His inner circle.

Abraham believed God. That's it.

Abraham didn't treat God's promises like some pie-in-the-sky, never-gonna-happen pipe dreams. He *believed* God. As in, if God said it, it would happen. Abraham's actions matched his beliefs. That kind of faith and loyalty to God is rare. But when it happens, it makes God so happy. He pulls that person right in close and says, "I like you. Let's be buddies."

God loves all His children. He knows we struggle with faith sometimes. But when we give up our fears and doubts and trust Him with abandon, something special happens. Our relationship shifts. And He calls us *friend*.

I'm so grateful to be Your child, Father. But I want more than that. I want to be Your friend. Teach me to believe like Abraham believed.

COMING ALIVE

For as the body apart from the spirit is dead,
so also faith apart from works is dead.
JAMES 2:26

When someone is truly alive, they do things. A person who is fully alive breathes, speaks, and moves. They have relationships and responsibilities. They laugh, cry, and eat chocolate. But if someone is severely depressed and won't get out of bed, they stop acting and doing. We might say that person isn't really living. They're certainly not living a full life. And if someone is in the hospital, in a coma, being kept alive by a ventilator, we might question how much living that person is doing. We'd pray that they would wake up and walk away from the ventilator so they could experience more life.

Many of us are physically alive, but our faith is on a ventilator. We say we believe God's promises. . .we may even warm a pew on Sunday mornings. But our actions don't match our words. We're devastated when we lose our job instead of trusting that God will take care of all our needs. We manipulate situations to our advantage instead of believing God has everything under control. We spend our lives pursuing more money, more status, and more comfort instead of pouring out our lives in love. And we wonder why we feel dead inside.

Is your faith on a ventilator? If so, remove it and get to work. When your actions match your professed belief in God, you will feel more alive than ever.

Help me come alive in You, Father.

TWO KINDS OF WISDOM

For where jealousy and selfish ambition exist, there will be disorder and every vile practice. But the wisdom from above is first pure, then peaceable, gentle, open to reason, full of mercy and good fruits, impartial and sincere. And a harvest of righteousness is sown in peace by those who make peace.

JAMES 3:16–18

James makes a stark contrast between worldly wisdom and God's wisdom. Worldly wisdom says to get ahead at all costs. Look out for number one. All's fair in love and war. Worldly wisdom says if we're not first, we're not successful. It promotes jealousy and self-centeredness in hopes of being important. But that kind of wisdom leads to lying, cheating, and manipulation.

God's wisdom is the opposite and goes against human nature. It says to put others first. It encourages love and self-sacrifice. It puts humility ahead of self-promotion and kindness ahead of success. God's wisdom promotes peace by showing love, compassion, and mercy. When we sow these seeds of peace, we'll end up with a cornucopia of righteousness and every good gift that comes from God.

We can use worldly wisdom to seek worldly power and riches and success. The sad thing is, whether we get those things or not, Satan will use that kind of ladder-climbing to destroy us. Or we can embrace God's wisdom, which brings joy, peace, contentment, and a rich, abundant life.

I'm sorry for getting pulled into worldly wisdom. Give me Your wisdom, Lord, and teach me to follow it.

WHO WE ARE

As obedient children, do not be conformed to the passions of your former ignorance, but as he who called you is holy, you also be holy in all your conduct, since it is written, "You shall be holy, for I am holy."
1 PETER 1:14–16

Everyone who has chosen Christ, who has accepted His gift of salvation, has a past. There was a time when we *didn't* have Christ and we lived for ourselves. It's part of being human. A baby or small child cries when hungry and often throws a fit when they don't get their way. They're not thinking about Mom being tired or Dad not having enough money to buy that toy. We're all self-centered by nature. It's who we are.

The directive to be holy like God may sound discouraging. After all, none of us can be perfect like God. Yet the definition of *holy* is "set apart." We won't reach a sinless state until we're in heaven. But we *can* separate ourselves from the world. We can choose to live a life of faith, not selfishness. When we accept Christ, we become part of God's family. We are His children, holy and set apart. This command to be holy isn't an impossible task. He's simply asking us to be who we already are in Christ.

Thank You for making me holy and setting me aside as Yours. Help me make daily choices to set myself apart as I imitate You.

LIFE CHANGER

His divine power has granted to us all things that pertain to life and godliness, through the knowledge of him who called us to his own glory and excellence, by which he has granted to us his precious and very great promises, so that through them you may become partakers of the divine nature, having escaped from the corruption that is in the world because of sinful desire.

2 PETER 1:3–4

Living a godly life is hard, especially in this age of social media and constant access to all manner of ungodliness right at our fingertips. Some may wonder if it's even possible to live a life that pleases God anymore. But God has given us everything we need to live an upright, holy life. The pantry is full. All we have to do is open the doors and use what has already been provided. But here's the catch: He's promised to give us what we need, but how can we access those things if we don't know what they are? To take advantage of His promises, we have to know them.

The more ungodliness we let into our minds, the more ungodly choices we'll make. The more of God's Word we saturate ourselves with, the more we'll claim His promises of peace, joy, patience, strength, and everything else we need to live like a child of God.

Read His Word. Think about it. Meditate on it. It will change your life.

**Thank You for Your promises, Father.
Help me incorporate them into my life.**

MAKE EVERY EFFORT

For this very reason, make every effort to supplement your faith with virtue, and virtue with knowledge, and knowledge with self-control, and self-control with steadfastness, and steadfastness with godliness, and godliness with brotherly affection, and brotherly affection with love.

2 Peter 1:5–7

Faith in God gives us such a strong start for everything we do. But faith is just the *starting point*. It's like the basic bundle, when God wants us to have the VIP package. As we grow in our faith, other benefits are added. We become more virtuous. We gain wisdom and self-control. We become loyal and godly and kind.

We become more *loving*.

Peter urges his listeners not to settle for the basic package. He wants them (and us) to *make every effort* to add these qualities to our lives. That means we'll mess up. We'll fail sometimes. Even so, we're not to give up. Making every effort means trying as many times as it takes to learn those new traits. In the process, our faith will be supersized.

> I've tried to be godly, Father. I've tried to be kind and self-controlled, patient and virtuous. But I'm just not very good at it sometimes. Each time I fail, I want to give up. I tell myself, "That's just the way I am." Help me make every effort to become who You want me to be.

MISSING THE POINT

For if these qualities are yours and are increasing, they keep you from being ineffective or unfruitful in the knowledge of our Lord Jesus Christ. For whoever lacks these qualities is so nearsighted that he is blind, having forgotten that he was cleansed from his former sins.

2 PETER 1:8–9

In the previous verses, Peter told his readers that God has already given them all the tools they need to live a godly life. They're right there, ready to be used. But we don't become experts in their use by osmosis. We must *practice*. We must make *every effort* to become good at using the traits and tools God has provided.

Here in verse 8, Peter goes a step further. He says if we *don't* use these tools God has given us, we're missing the point of being a Christian. It's like having millions of dollars in the bank and living as a pauper, simply because we're too lazy to make a withdrawal. We don't want to put in the effort. In the moment, it's easier to live penniless.

Such shortsightedness seems ridiculous when we think of money. But God's gifts are so much more valuable than earthly treasure. Godliness and all the traits that come with it have value both here and for eternity.

Help me use the tools You've given me to grow in faith and godliness, Father. I'd rather pursue You than anything else in this world.

WALK

And by this we know that we have come to know him, if we keep his commandments. Whoever says "I know him" but does not keep his commandments is a liar, and the truth is not in him, but whoever keeps his word, in him truly the love of God is perfected. By this we may know that we are in him: whoever says he abides in him ought to walk in the same way in which he walked.

1 JOHN 2:3–6

Wow. Pretty strong language here. If we love Jesus, we'll keep His commandments. If we don't keep His commandments, we're liars and we don't actually know Him.

John is not advocating for salvation by works. We all mess up—even mature Christians stumble. John says if we abide in Christ, we should walk the same way Christ walks. It may help to picture yourself walking on a path. No matter how careful you are, you may trip over a root and stumble. It could happen to anyone. But if you get back up and keep walking, you're still making the journey toward your destination.

In contrast, if you turn around and walk the other way, you've chosen a different path. When we walk like Christ walked, we stay on His path. When we sin, we admit we messed up and keep going. But if we consistently choose a way of life that defies Christ's commands and His character, we must ask ourselves if our commitment is real.

Walk with Christ or away from Him. The choice is yours.

I love You, Lord. I want to walk like You walk.

INVESTMENT

Do not love the world or the things in the world. If anyone loves the world, the love of the Father is not in him. For all that is in the world—the desires of the flesh and the desires of the eyes and pride of life—is not from the Father but is from the world. And the world is passing away along with its desires, but whoever does the will of God abides forever.
1 JOHN 2:15–17

If someone gave you a thousand dollars, how would you spend it? Some might throw a party or buy new clothes. Others might invest it in a solid mutual fund. Ten years from now, the first may barely remember the party, and the new clothes will be old and threadbare. The second person will still have the original investment and more.

John is urging us to invest this life—these years we have on earth—wisely. If we focus on fleshly desires (like food or sexual immorality), that immediate gratification is short-lived. If we focus on "desires of the eyes," or material things, those items—and our enjoyment of them—will wear out. And if we focus on our pride, trying to impress others and bring attention to ourselves, we head down an endless rabbit hole. We'll never be satisfied. None of those things last.

But when we love God with our *whole hearts*, our desires change. We want to please Him because we're so grateful for His love. When we live for God and do His will, we reap benefits both now and for eternity.

I love You, Father. I want to invest my life in You.

PERMANENT ADDRESS

But the anointing that you received from him abides in you, and you have no need that anyone should teach you. But as his anointing teaches you about everything, and is true, and is no lie—just as it has taught you, abide in him.

1 JOHN 2:27

The "anointing" John refers to is the Holy Spirit. When we choose to follow Christ, the Holy Spirit moves into our lives. He's not just visiting. He *abides* in us. Your heart becomes His permanent address. When we truly seek Him, He becomes our teacher. He shows us things we previously missed before we became Christians. He gives us wisdom and discernment we didn't have before. God's Word and His Holy Spirit are really all we need.

This doesn't mean we shouldn't learn from pastors and teachers and people who have been Christians longer than we have. But John previously warned against false teachers. When we have the Holy Spirit, He will let us know when someone isn't preaching or teaching the truth. We'll know it in our spirits, and we will be able to confirm it through God's Word.

The Holy Spirit is real. He is a gift, given to each person who chooses Christ. Yet many don't take the time to get to know Him. Many brush off His counsel, choosing instead to listen to popular logic and worldly wisdom. Just as the Holy Spirit abides (or lives) in us, we should make His presence our permanent address.

Thank You for abiding in me, Father. I want to abide in You.

LOVE

Beloved, let us love one another, for love is from God, and whoever loves has been born of God and knows God. Anyone who does not love does not know God, because God is love. In this the love of God was made manifest among us, that God sent his only Son into the world, so that we might live through him. In this is love, not that we have loved God but that he loved us and sent his Son to be the propitiation for our sins. Beloved, if God so loved us, we also ought to love one another.

1 JOHN 4:7–11

John urges us to love each other because love is from God. He goes on to say that if we don't love, we don't even know God, because God *is* love. Think about that.

God equals love. They are one and the same.

God cannot hate a person. He hates sin, but only because sin destroys the people He created, the people He loves so much. If God cannot hate, and He lives in us, it stands to reason we can't hate either. God won't tolerate hate, because He is love. He is so complete, so passionate in His love, that He gave His Son to die so that we might be saved.

Christians may be *tempted* to hate. But if God truly lives in us, we'll be miserable if we entertain or give in to that temptation. God will urge us to forgive, to reconcile, to *love*. We are, after all, made in His image. Love is a defining feature of His children.

Thank You for loving me, Lord. Help me love like You do.

OVERCOMER

For everyone who has been born of God overcomes the world.
And this is the victory that has overcome the world—our faith.

1 JOHN 5:4

This verse is like a coach's pep talk before the big game. The "game" is every day of our lives here on earth. We're players in an epic battle, and it's made even more exciting because we already know the ending—and we're on the winning team.

We are the winners, the victors, the overcomers! Christ has already won. But we get to join Him in the conquest by playing our parts. What makes us so strong? What makes us overcomers?

It's our faith in Jesus Christ.

When we leave our faith behind, it's like walking into a battle tired and hungry, with no energy and no armor. That's when we end up feeling like victims, losers, and failures. That's what Satan wants us to think. But the minute we strap on our faith, we are supercharged with power—not our own power, but Christ's power in us.

Hebrews 11:1 tells us that faith is believing without seeing. It's treating hope as reality. It's acting as if something already is, even though we haven't seen it yet. We know God is real because we feel His presence in our lives. We can look backward and see all the amazing things He's done. So for the believer, faith is reasonable. It is solid. And we can live each day as overcomers because God has said we are. And His Word is true.

Thank You for making me an overcomer, Lord. Remind me to live like one.

LOVE LIFE

*"But I have this complaint against you.
You don't love me or each other as you did at first!"*
REVELATION 2:4 NLT

This section of Revelation addresses the Christians at Ephesus. They've disappointed God because they no longer live a life of love—either for God or for each other. Without love, the Christian life is pretty pointless.

Imagine a parent who provides for their child's basic needs but only out of a sense of obligation and not love. That child will probably grow up feeling rejected and unlovable. What if a husband leaves his wife, sending money back home for groceries and rent but never interacting with her or showing her that he loves her? That marriage will feel stale and cold. Love is what gives our relationships power and longevity. It's what makes life worthwhile.

So how must God feel when we go through the motions of faith but without any real feeling or passion? He commends our obedience. . . but He wants our *hearts*. He'd rather we love Him sincerely but imperfectly than that we follow every rule without spending time with Him or worshipping Him. He created us to *love*. In Matthew 22:37–39, Christ tells us the first commandment is to love God with our whole hearts, and the second is to love our neighbors as we love ourselves.

How is your love life?

Father, I'm sorry for going through the motions without letting love be the driving force. Reignite my love for You and others.

THE SHARPEST SWORD

From his mouth came a sharp sword to strike down the nations. He will rule them with an iron rod. He will release the fierce wrath of God, the Almighty, like juice flowing from a winepress.
REVELATION 19:15 NLT

These words paint a startling contrast to Christ's first appearance on earth. The first time, He came as a tiny, helpless baby. When He comes again, He'll show up as a fierce warrior. When we're called overcomers, this is what that means. We're on the winning team.

In the meantime, we're in a battle. That sharp sword mentioned in this verse? Hebrews 4:12 tells us God's Word is sharper than any two-edged sword. Ephesians 6 tells us God's Word is the sword of the Spirit. In that final battle, Jesus will overcome using the sharpest sword ever. The author describes the sword coming from Jesus' mouth. . .it's the Word of God! Isn't that cool?

And here's something even cooler. We can fight with the *same sword*. We have God's Word. The more we read it, study it, meditate on it, digest it, and memorize it, the more accessible it becomes. If you feel defeated, grab hold of your sword. Satan cannot win against God's Word.

I can't believe I've neglected Your Word, Lord. It's my defense, my offense, my lifeline. Help me make time to read Your Word and learn all Your promises. I want my sword to be sharp.

GIVE CREDIT

Ascribe to the LORD, O heavenly beings, ascribe to the LORD glory and strength. Ascribe to the LORD the glory due his name; worship the LORD in the splendor of holiness.
PSALM 29:1–2

The word *ascribe* means to give credit to someone as the cause or source of something. It's the opposite of plagiarism, which is withholding credit from its rightful source or taking the credit for something that isn't yours. David encourages the "heavenly beings," or angels, to give credit to God for glory and strength.

A *scribe* is an official person who writes things down, creating permanent records. So when we ascribe something, we give credit in an official, permanent way. It's important that we Christians become official scribes of God's glory. We need to give Him credit for all the great things He has done in our lives.

It's one thing to *think* about God's goodness. We may thank Him silently for His help, His strength, His wisdom, and His blessings. He loves when we talk to Him, even in our thoughts. But it's essential to share those things so others can know of His goodness too. Write in a journal to share with your children. Make posts on social media. Tell your stories out loud. Give credit to God—ascribe to Him the goodness and glory He deserves.

Thank You for sharing all Your good qualities with me, Father. I am overwhelmed. Make me bold to share Your glory with others. I want everyone to know how amazing You are.

INFLUENCE

Blessed is the man who walks not in the counsel of the wicked, nor stands in the way of sinners, nor sits in the seat of scoffers; but his delight is in the law of the Lord, and on his law he meditates day and night. He is like a tree planted by streams of water that yields its fruit in its season, and its leaf does not wither. In all that he does, he prospers.
Psalm 1:1–3

American businessman and success coach Dan Peña said, "Show me your friends and I'll show you your future." He went on to clarify that when we hang around with people who have no ambition, who make bad choices, or who look for trouble, that's who we'll become. But if we choose friends who have high standards, who work hard and are honest, and who set their minds on higher things, that's the kind of person we'll turn out to be. This idea isn't a new one. Way back in biblical times, the psalmist said basically the same thing.

If we choose to hang around wicked, rebellious people, we'll become the same way. But when we delight in God, spend time in His Word, and cherish our time talking with Him in prayer, He becomes our best friend. Then His standards become our standards, and we become good examples for others to follow as we follow Him. If you want to be prosperous in every way that counts, hang around with God and the people who love Him.

Help me stay away from people who will lead me down the wrong paths, Lord. You are my best friend, and I delight in You.

WAIT FOR THE LORD

Our soul waits for the Lord; he is our help and our shield.
For our heart is glad in him, because we trust in his holy name.
PSALM 33:20 21

In today's fast-paced society, we don't like to wait. We want a fresh, home-cooked meal, and we want it now. We want personal, friendly service, but we don't want to wait in line while *others* receive personal, friendly service. Waiting requires patience, which is a rare commodity these days.

Time and again in God's Word, He tells us to *wait* on Him. We humans tend to be self-centered, focused on our own wants and needs. Like newborn infants, we throw a fit if we don't see immediate results. Yet God has a better plan. He sees a bigger picture. He's doing something so much greater than we can imagine. But permanent, lasting outcomes take time. He refuses to give us fast-food fixes when He can provide five-star results.

Trust Him. Be glad for what He's doing in your life. And be patient, knowing He is worth the wait.

I'm not good at waiting, Lord. I want results, and I want them now. Forgive me for being childish and bossy in my requests. I trust Your goodness, Your plan, and Your love for me. I'm so grateful for what You're doing. Teach me to wait.

WAITING WITH HOPE

*Let your steadfast love, O Lord,
be upon us, even as we hope in you.*
PSALM 33:22

Hope is the exact opposite of fear and anxiety. Hope is the belief that good things are in store. Fear is the belief that something bad is coming. Though God tells us over and over in His Word that He is hope, though He reminds us to hope in Him, many of us are ruled by fear.

Second Timothy 1:7 tells us that God didn't give us a spirit of fear. Fear is not from God! Countless times, He tells us not to be afraid. Countless times, He reminds us to hope in Him. That means we're supposed to look toward the future with expectations of good things coming and without fear of bad things. God is kind. He loves His children. And He has good things in store.

When we don't understand our circumstances, when we question what's happening and what He's doing in our lives, we can trust His steadfast love. We can trust His heart for us. We can face all our tomorrows with joy and peace and *hope*.

Heavenly Father, too often my mind spins into doomsday mode. I think of all the bad things that could happen, and I wait expectantly for the worst. But I realize that attitude is not from You. Help me shift my mindset to one of hope in You. I know You love me, and I can wait with a smile on my face for the good things You have in store.

RECIPE FOR A LONG, PROSPEROUS LIFE

Come, O children, listen to me; I will teach you the fear of the LORD. What man is there who desires life and loves many days, that he may see good? Keep your tongue from evil and your lips from speaking deceit. Turn away from evil and do good; seek peace and pursue it.
PSALM 34:11–14

It's important for Christians to understand the difference between a principle and a promise. In these verses, David writes about principles. These are general rules. Sometimes there are exceptions. Someone may do all these things and still die young. But our chances for a long, prosperous life are much better if we follow these standards:

- Fear God. This isn't the same kind of fear that accompanies anxiety. Instead, this kind of fear is a deep respect and awe of God as our Creator, Master, Father, and King.
- Guard your tongue. Don't gossip, slander, use offensive language, or tell lies. Use your words for good and not evil.
- Run from evil.
- Do as much good as you can.
- Seek peace and do all you can to pursue good relationships with those around you and with God. Keep peace in your home by refusing to allow chaos.

Do these things and God will bless your efforts to live in a way that pleases Him.

Help me avoid evil and live a godly life, Lord.

RESTORED

He restores my soul. He leads me in paths of righteousness for his name's sake.
PSALM 23:3

An expert in car restoration often takes old, run-down vehicles and brings them back to a new state. The idea of restoration tells us that time, hardship, and even abuse have caused wear and tear. If nothing bad had happened, there'd be no need for restoration.

God knows the process of living this life will cause some damage. Sin leaves scars. Satan's goal is to destroy us. Ephesians 6:12 tells us we all face a spiritual struggle, a battle. Battles leave us banged up and bruised, empty and exhausted.

But God *restores our souls*. He makes us new again. No matter what sin does to us—whether our own sin or others' abuse—God will make it right. He will heal our spirits. He will use our experiences to make us stronger, wiser, and more like Him.

Are you weary? Do you carry scars and bruises? Sink into His presence and let Him restore you. He will make you better than new.

Thank You for this promise of restoration, Father. I'm exhausted. Some days I feel like I just can't face another thing. Each step is a struggle. But I know You won't leave me that way forever. Right now, I want to lean my head on Your great shoulder and rest. Restore my soul.

OUT LOUD

*Proclaiming thanksgiving aloud,
and telling all your wondrous deeds.*

PSALM 26:7

Have you ever done something nice for someone, and they didn't thank you? How did that make you feel? God does thoughtful, wonderful, generous things for us every day. Too often we take those things for granted and forget to thank Him.

If we were to thank God for every single blessing, we wouldn't be able to accomplish much else. His goodness is overwhelming! But we can take a moment to thank Him out loud, in front of others, so He gets the glory for the good things in our lives.

When we share His kindnesses with the people around us, we actually point them to Him. If they don't know Him, our words stir their curiosity, and they may seek Him for themselves. Jeremiah 29:13 tells us that when we seek the Lord with all our hearts, we will find Him. So by thanking God for His goodness out loud so others can hear, we may start a chain reaction that leads others to Christ.

I have so many things to thank You for, Father. Your goodness overwhelms me. I'm sorry for taking Your blessings for granted. Open up opportunities for me to share Your love with others by giving You credit for the good things in my life. Give me boldness to thank You out loud. I'm so grateful for all You do for me.

THE LAND OF THE LIVING

I believe that I shall look upon the goodness of the Lord in the land of the living! Wait for the Lord; be strong, and let your heart take courage; wait for the Lord!
Psalm 27:13–14

David, the author of this psalm, went through some awful times. After he saved Israel by killing Goliath, King Saul became jealous. David eventually had to flee, hiding in caves and enduring bad weather and hunger. Later, David's own son challenged him for the throne. These are just a few of the many hardships David faced. Yet he knew and trusted that God was good, every step of the way.

It's easy to think of our rewards in heaven and forget about the rewards God gives us here and now. But God's goodness exists in the land of the living. We often must wait, for patience is a virtue that pleases God. Sometimes He's putting things in place—things that take time—to bless us in ways we never could have imagined.

When you face hard times, remind yourself of this verse. Say it out loud: "I will look on God's goodness in this lifetime." Like David, wait with expectancy. God loves you, and He has amazing things in store for your life.

Your promises give me strength, Father. I know You love me, and I can't wait to see what You're doing behind the scenes while I wait. I know I will experience so much more of Your goodness in this life!

SCRIPTURE INDEX

OLD TESTAMENT

Deuteronomy
31:8 16

2 Chronicles
7:13–14 11

Psalm
1:1–3 182
19:7–11 9
23:3 186
23:4 17
26:7 187
27:1 10
27:13–14 188
29:1–2 181
33:20–21 183
33:22 184
34:4 14
34:11–14 185

Isaiah
41:10 13

NEW TESTAMENT

Mark
1:40–42 19
1:43–45 20
3:11 21
3:20–21 22
4:39 23
5:18–20 24
6:27–29 25
6:34 26
6:56 27
7:37 28
8:36–37 29
9:22–24 30
9:35 31
10:13–14 32
10:21–22 33
10:32–34 34
10:51–52 35
11:2 36
11:12–14 37
12:18, 23 38
12:30–31 39
13:10 40
16:3–4 41
16:7 42
16:9 43

16:20 44

LUKE
1:18–20 45
1:49–50 46
2:14 47
2:19–20 48
2:36–38 49
2:40 50
3:11 51
4:5–7 52
4:18–19, 28–29 53
5:4–6 55
5:15–16 56
5:18–20 57
6:6–7, 11 54
6:19 58
7:39, 50 59
8:24–25 60
9:2–4 61
9:18–20 62
10:1–2 63
10:40–42 64
12:11–12 65
12:58–59 66
13:14–16 67
14:26 68
14:34–35 69
19:8–9 70
19:26 71
20:23–25 72
20:45–47 73

22:10–13 74
23:11 75
23:22–25 76
23:26 77
24:10–11 78

JOHN
1:1–5 79
1:38–39 80
1:47–48 81
7:37–38 82
8:34–36 83
10:10 84
11:5–6 85
11:38–41 86
14:27 12
15:7–9 87
18:10–11 88
18:33–36 89
19:38–39 90

ACTS
4:32 91
5:1–2 92
8:1–3 93
11:29–30 94
12:4–5 95
15:30–32 96
15:38–41 97
17:4, 12 98
20:24 99
27:1 100
27:42–43 101

Romans

1:16–17	102
2:13	103
2:28–29	104
4:3, 18–22	105
8:5–8	107
8:31, 35, 37	108
8:38–39	109
10:17	110
11:22–23	111
11:33	112
12:1–2	113
12:3–5	114
12:6–8	115
12:9–13	116
12:14–16	117
12:17–19	118
12:20–21	119
13:12–14	120
14:4	121
14:22–23	122
15:13	123
16:19	124

1 Corinthians

1:26–27	125
2:1–2	126
6:9–11	127
9:24–27	128
15:42–44	129
16:14	130
16:17–18	131

2 Corinthians

3:5–6, 17	132
6:17–18	133
9:6–7	134
10:17–18	135
13:11	136

Galatians

5:16–17	137
5:22–23	138

Ephesians

3:17–19	139
3:20–21	140
4:1–3	141
4:11–13	142
4:30–32	143
6:10–13	144

Philippians

1:22–24	145
2:3–8	146
3:10	147
4:6–7	15
4:8–9	148
4:11–13	149

Colossians

4:2	150

1 Thessalonians

4:16–18	151
5:16–18	152

1 Timothy

1:1–2	153
6:10–11	154

2 Timothy

1:16–18	155
2:22–25	156
3:1–5	157
4:7–8	158
4:16–18	159

Hebrews

2:17–18	160
10:23–25	161
10:35–36	162
11:1	18
11:6	106
13:15–17	163

James

1:1	164
1:26	165
1:27	166
2:23	167
2:26	168
3:16–18	169

1 Peter

1:14–16	170

2 Peter

1:3–4	171
1:5–7	172
1:8–9	173

1 John

2:3–6	174
2:15–17	175
2:27	176
4:7–11	177
5:4	178

Revelation

2:4	179
19:15	180